RIDING FOR
THE GOLD,
NATURALLY

*Lauren
Barwick's
Incredible
Journey*

Susan
O'Brien

About The Author

Susan O'Brien taught in Middle School for 31 years. She taught English, creative writing, journalism, drama as well as other subjects in the humanities. She produced the school newspaper and plays that kept her students engaged and energized. Her love of the written word earned her an award from the Greater San Diego Reading Association as an "Outstanding Teacher of Reading/Language Arts". She is a graduate of San Diego State University with a degree in English and Drama. She continued on to earn a teaching credential at SDSU and then completed her master's degree in Educational Psychology at United States International University. But before all this, she developed a life-long love of horses. Because of this passion, she pursued excellence in her horsemanship in Parelli Natural Horsemanship. Attending a conference in Pagosa Springs, Colorado, at the Parelli Ranch she was introduced to an incredible athlete named Lauren Barwick. Lauren's life story and talent as a rider as well as her dream to go to the Summer Olympics in 2008 peaked Susan's interest. She contacted Lauren and followed her incredible journey through to the Olympics and back through her childhood, the accident that took her from able-bodied rider in eventing and show jumping to Para-Equestrian and later Paralympian. She and Lauren have worked closely to create a biography that is not only true to fact but engaging and often surprising. Contact the author at ridingforgold naturally.intuitwebsites.com

Acknowledgments

This book has truly been a labor of love. I want to thank those I love, those who love me, and the six loving horses in our lives that have helped to make this story possible. I also need to give a shout out to our two dogs, two birds and one cat whose love and silliness keep me grounded. Bill O'Brien, the love of my life, has patiently listened to my ideas, calmly helped me avoid meltdowns, generously helped me travel to meet with Lauren and most importantly introduced me to Parelli Natural Horsemanship facilitating my introduction to not only Lauren, but a whole new way to understand and have fun with my horses. Bill's love and support has given me an opportunity to write in a creative environment and our mutual love for our horses, the centerpiece of our life together, has spurred me forward. My dear friend, Susan Heaney, the best writer I know, helped me greatly with editing. She took time away from her precious grandchildren and goat farm to support me with this project. She is the epitome of true friendship. I love her so much. I want to thank my horses who didn't always get to play with Mom or get ridden because I was writing, but I always knew I could talk to them and they would understand! I want to thank my daughter, Myria, for assisting me with all things "tech", watching the ranch while we were taking trips to Parelli events, and for her unconditional love and encouragement. She has always been my number one fan. I want to thank Pat and Linda Parelli for their Natural Horsemanship Program that makes this world a better place for horses and the people who love them. Lastly, I owe a huge debt of gratitude to Lauren Barwick for being who she is, an incredible model for living a full life with courage, zest, and purpose. Her story, the story I was writing, inspired me to keep on keeping on when the going seemed difficult. I couldn't quit. Lauren never did!

"Don't let what you cannot do interfere with what you can do."

COACH JOHN WOODEN

Prologue

Standing on the edge of a new year and her lifelong dream, a young promising athlete gazes out at a future filled with hope and overwhelming challenges. Lauren Barwick has moved from British Columbia, Canada, to the Parelli Ranch in Ocala, Florida, but the quest has remained the same...the Olympic Games, 2008. She has been qualified to ride dressage for the Canadian Team, but she doesn't have a qualified horse. This and so many other trials will begin the year 2008 and follow her all the way to Hong Kong, where the Olympic Equestrian Games will be staged.

Having spent time in Colorado with Pat and Linda Parelli, and immersing herself in the Parelli Natural Horsemanship Program, Lauren feels they can help her find a horse and offer her the support she needs to go all the way. Their patronage has enabled her to leave her job with the Royal Bank of Canada and travel to Florida to continue showing, training and shopping for a horse. The pressure is on. June 4, 2008, is the final date to submit qualifying scores for the horse or horses a rider selects to take. Lauren has been training on a lovely Andulusian-Thoroughbred cross mare named River that belongs to the Parellis. At the British Columbia Provincials in May of 2007, Lauren won two silver medals her first go on River and is optimistic that this is the horse to move her closer to her destination. Arriving back from phenomenal performances with Pat in Australia, River doesn't appear to be consistently sound enough to pass the rigorous checks by the veterinarians at the Olympic Games, and the sad decision is made to not take her. Lauren tearfully tells her the news that she won't be going to "the party of a lifetime", as Lauren describes the 2008 Games, and begins the search for the horse that could take her to her dream.

For any equestrian finding the perfect horse can be a formidable task. For an elite athlete with Lauren's high aspirations and her sights set on gold, this can be overwhelming. But Lauren understands meeting and overcoming obstacles. She's been there before. She will need a special horse. One who can adapt to the greatest obstacle Lauren has ever faced, being paralyzed from the waist down. Yes, Lauren became a paraplegic at the age of twenty-two after spending years as an accomplished able-bodied rider. She knows this special horse is out there somewhere just waiting for her.

If they haven't already, baffling questions have to come up at this point. How does she communicate with her horse? How does she handle the difficulties of getting on and off a horse without the use of her legs? How does she saddle a horse? How does she stay on? How does she do it, emotionally and physically? The answers to these questions are to be found in the incredible story of her life. Not just in 2008, but in her entire life. The accident that left her a paraplegic is just the climax to a life filled with challenges that have pummeled Lauren with questions of her own and created in her an indomitable spirit. So it's back to Canada for the Canadian Nationals for the last qualifying score. Filled with trepidation, it's back to the home of her birth near Vancouver, back to the landmark of the injury that so absolutely altered the course of her life.

LAUREN RIDING RIVER 2006

Chapter 1

Like a quilt, events in our lives are stitched together one piece at a time; fragments of cloth sewn carefully, sometimes lovingly, sometimes not, but certainly each informing the whole. Looking at the pieces in Lauren's life, it is obvious that her quilt is going to be colorful, spectacular and perhaps a little torn at the edges.

Lauren came into this world September 12, 1977, eleven months behind a younger brother who was born with a heart problem that consequently resulted in severe brain damage. Cameron was never able to walk, talk or move so Lauren's mother cared for him at home all of his short life. He died at the age of twenty-two in his sleep. Partly because of her brother's tragic circumstances, Lauren's mother and father never married, and in fact separated before Lauren was born. Lauren was raised by both her mother, Gail Barwick, and father, Ray Smith, in separate homes, finding qualities in both parents that shaped her life. Her father helped to ground her and gave her people skills while her mother blessed her with the ability to adapt to life, to be spontaneous, and most importantly, to think outside the box.

Lauren's mother was married and later divorced from Lauren's younger sister's father. Rosemary, the younger sister, was born in 1984 with Down Syndrome. She is still living at home, is highly functioning, and works in a local restaurant. Lauren, growing up with two disabled siblings and a single mother, ironically, has always been the "normal one". Despite this apparent "normality", she experienced first-hand the physical and emotional struggles that disabilities in family members afford the family as a whole. Life for Lauren's mom, in particular, was hard. Lauren was frightened at the way her mom appeared to be treated by society, and because of this, Lauren felt like an outcast as well. Nevertheless Lauren learned some valuable lessons that would benefit her later in the midst of her own physical challenges. Life doesn't give guarantees to anyone, including parents, she realized. Every human being and family can be affected by some kind of life altering disaster or disease. It seems to defy the odds that later Lauren would find herself a paraplegic.

The beautiful little community of Aldergrove, located in British Columbia, was Lauren's home from birth until fourth grade. These years were spent primarily with her mother, Cameron and Rosemary. Lots of animals were on the farm she grew up on. Lauren showed goats in 4H and even traveled with Mom to California to show them. An especially fond memory, this California trip stands out for its mishaps as well as the fun. After a painful mosquito attack, Lauren's mom, with a recommendation from one of the carnies, gave her Preparation H to bring down the swelling. Lauren also remembers falling asleep in the truck with gum in her mouth and getting it stuck in her hair. Reluctantly Lauren relates a story about going up to a vendor, on this same trip, and telling him she was on welfare. Feeling sorry for the little girl, the vendor gave her free popsicles. When Mom found out, she immediately repaid him. During her childhood,

Lauren's mom took her to her favorite stores to buy olives, and they picked pomegranates together. From grand trips to places such as Disneyland and the Redwoods, to the very, very simple, her mom created an exciting adventure, unique and educational, each time she was with Lauren, just for the two of them.

At Christmastime, the family would make gingerbread houses together. They froze water on the trampoline, and Lauren would go outside and smash it with a hammer. This would create big blocks of ice to make homemade ice cream. In the summer, the trampoline would provide even more fun. Lauren would put soap and bubbles on it and jump and slide around. Lauren recalls she lost a lot of teeth on that trampoline. Instruments of all kinds, a trumpet, a piano, a harmonica and drums, were available in Lauren's home to experiment with. Even though Lauren's mom was single and not working, Lauren grew up in a colorful environment, and looking back, she realizes that she got to experience more than a lot of children do. Lauren participated in Brownies and Girl Guides. Despite living on welfare, Lauren had diverse and interesting opportunities. She went to a private Christian school, a public school and because Mom was highly educated, was also home-schooled. In fourth grade, Lauren's mom bought a house and they moved. Lauren attended a public elementary school and then things got a little messy.

Children do fall down and get hurt. This is common. But it doesn't always alter a child's life like one fall from a ladder did Lauren's. She was badly bruised from the fall, and the school called in social services. Lauren was asked if her mother hit her. Being honest, Lauren said yes because she did get spanked. But nervous and upset, she didn't mention the ladder. Lauren was taken away and put in a foster home where there was abuse, more than she had seen in her life. She was not abused there, but it was a horrible place for her to be. Lauren would have had to stay in this home a long time before her mother could get things straightened out in court, so Gail gave Lauren's father, Ray, full custody. Lauren would live with him and Ray's wife, Robin, for the next four years and be moved again.

Her new home, at the age of nine, became Sointula, an island off of Vancouver. Lauren feels some of her real development took place here, and she remembers this island as a great place to grow up. Ray and Robin lived on a beautiful fourteen acre farm on Mahlm's Pond. But it also could be described as more like camping than anything else. The house was heated by a wood stove on the main floor so on cold nights everyone needed to bring mattresses down to the living room and sleep by the fire. The plumbing frequently froze, there was a plastic bag over the chimney to keep in heat and the windows were cracked. Lauren learned to split kindling to get the wood stove burning.

One vivid memory she has of her father comes to her as a rainy day and Dad, as usual, is making her lunch for school. Despite the pouring rain, he went outside with a ladder and picked red plums for her snack. That's how her dad was. She played baseball, practicing with a pitching net and mound, rode horses her mother had sent up to Sointula and fished. She had karate lessons, painting lessons and piano lessons. Here she got a taste of what she calls a normal household for 1986. Lauren attributes her father, acting as a role model, with accelerating her social skills and helping her to develop confidence.

They butted heads about keeping her room clean, as most kids and parents do. Lauren hid her dirty clothes and her father insisted that she keep her room cleaned properly. This battle continued the entire time she was there with no clear winner. Despite this clash of wills, her dad enjoyed his daughter being there and being able to observe her closely and watch her mature. He reminisces fondly about cold, dark winter evenings listening outside the barn to Lauren having conversations with her horses. He asked her once if she actually thought the horses understood what she was saying.

Looking at him in bewilderment, Lauren responded," Just because they are not talking back doesn't mean they don't understand. Sometimes, Dad, you don't answer me when I ask you questions."

Lauren remembers living with her dad and Robin as a good time in her life, but her dad never made it easy. He would not let her be a wimp. She was encouraged to "rub it off" as she says. Fishing, skiing or schooling, Lauren was taught the value of commitment and finishing what you start. She tells the story of never missing a day of school for the first two years she was with her dad. But the third year changed that. They were both working outside; he was cutting wood and she was stacking it. Lauren kept saying she felt sick and that her throat hurt. Her dad thought she was being over-dramatic and trying to get out of work. To his surprise, Lauren had tonsillitis and had to miss five days of school. He felt so badly, he brought her home ice cream every night. Lauren did learn perseverance and enjoyed her time on her dad's big farm where her friends could camp often, swim in the pond, hike and ice skate.

Ray and Robin, disappointingly unable to have children together, opened their home not only to Lauren, but foster children as well. Some would come just for the night and some would be there for a couple of months. Lauren's perspective on life was impacted seeing what life was like for other children, so many from broken homes for so many different reasons. When she was ten, two boys came to live with them, Jason, five, and his younger brother, Kyle who was three. They stayed with them long term, and Ray and Robin eventually adopted them. The struggles these boys went through because of their physical, emotional and mental abuse gave them a rough start in life which continues to be evident to this day. Having a unique way with them, Lauren babysat them and remembers them with fondness.

She kept in touch with her mother by phone, especially when she was upset by cruel actions or words coming from other kids. She continued to live in Sointula for grades four through seven until high school when she requested to return to her mother's. She hadn't realized that she was returning to some problems she thought she had left behind.

In the private Christian school Lauren had attended in elementary school, the students were required to wear a school uniform, grey skirts and white blouses. Lauren's mother made her wear these to public school as well. Lauren mentions that between the uniform and the two siblings with disabilities, children looked at her differently and this was tough. At the age of eight, Lauren remembers going home and explaining to her mother that all the kids had favorite singers and rock bands. Lauren's mom, with a background in classical and folk music, asked her who her favorite was. The only favorite Lauren could come up with was Willie Nelson singing *On the Road Again* from a children's show she watched. So Mom told her to tell the kids Willie Nelson was her favorite. Def Leopard and Bon Jovi were big back then, so the kids ridiculed her for her music choice as well. To further complicate her school life, Lauren was born dyslexic and had difficulty academically. Equally important, she found with her unusual upbringing and poor communication skills; she was having trouble making friends. Thought of as a different kid, odd, weird, she wanted to be accepted by other kids.

One Halloween stands out in Lauren's memory as a vivid example of why she didn't fit in at school. Gail created an elaborate costume comprised of a grass skirt and a staff. Spray painting Lauren black and covering her front with only beads, her mom told her to not talk because that was part of her costume and sent her to school. Among the other students' witch and pumpkin costumes, Lauren felt uncomfortable not just because she was shirtless, but because she stood out as an oddity. Her mother's eccentricity and her unusual childhood marked Lauren greatly and this would follow her into high school.

Now during this transition to eighth grade, she was seeing a lot of the same kids she had known in elementary. The transition to high school, difficult in the best of circumstances, was even harder for Lauren despite her beauty, blond hair, blue eyes and slim athletic build, because of her past history. Nevertheless, she did make a few good friends in ninth grade who she moved in with after graduating, Danielle, Leanne and Sandra. These friends would later provide her with lasting memories of house parties, trips, nightclubs, boyfriend troubles, car accidents and all the usual ups and downs that are part of a teenager's life.

An extremely unexpected occurrence in Lauren's teen years happened when she was seventeen. A sister she had never known about, half-sister to be exact, entered her life. Rachael was nineteen at the time, and the age at which her mother had agreed to tell her who her biological father was. It was Ray, Lauren's father. Rachael called Lauren a few times on the phone and then arranged to visit her at her mom's farmhouse. Rachael arrived wearing black jeans shorts and a black and white horizontally striped shirt. Lauren walked outside to meet her wearing black jeans and a black and white vertically striped shirt. It was an interesting feeling as Lauren recalls. More importantly they share some similar characteristics such as sarcasm, but Lauren tends to be more professional and competitive. Rachel, on the other hand, is more focused on her family including Lauren's one nephew and two lovely nieces.

Rachael became very supportive of Lauren's competitive equestrian career. For Athens, she made custom post cards with Lauren's picture on them and sold them for $20.00 each. They continue to keep in contact to this day.

Where do horses fit into this crazy childhood? Lauren has always been a horse lover, and her mother did her best to have horses around for her to ride as much as possible. At seven years old, Lauren's mother bought her a little black pony named Talka. Little did her mom know that this four-legged creature would totally influence her infatuation with horses such that it would become her passion in life.

As Lauren tells the story of Talka, "My little pony ran me down the fence, turned sharp corners and stopped from a full gallop, leaving me flying through the air landing with a thud in the hog fuel with tears streaming down my face. Why I kept getting on is beyond me."

I think she knows now why she has always kept getting back on. That is who she is. Determination and grit characterized Lauren early in her life. She competed in Pony Club for many years starting with three day eventing and then progressing to show jumping. For fun she participated in the Prince Philip Games, her team winning the Canadian Championships. She loved fox hunting with her mother. Running at a mad gallop across fields, through rivers, bending in and out of trees and jumping over whatever obstacle came their way she found exhilarating. The excitement was something she loved. She was one of the youngest riders to be awarded her colors, worn on the jacket collar to denote that the rider has been a contributing member to a particular fox hunt for some time. She was sixteen. Hounds as well as horses lived at the farm. While Lauren was focusing on jumping, she and her mom began breeding horses, and she was able to work with them from the time they were babies. Horses were her life. She loved the thrill of competition and accomplishment with her horse. All her future plans focused on horses, and then life took a different turn.

LAUREN'S FAMILY

LAUREN JUMPING PEANUT

Chapter 2

As a teenager, Lauren's goals and dreams fueled by ambition and a fierce competiveness moved her along the road to young adulthood. Dreams of becoming a great chef, or a great horsewoman, or a professional stunt person in the movies changed in the blink of an eye. One accident, turning her life on a 180 degree pivot, forced everything she'd dreamed of to become impossible from that moment in time.

In high school, Lauren had contemplated pursuing either the culinary arts, dramatic arts or continuing her childhood dream of competing as a professional equestrian. After graduating high school and suffering from teenage growing pains as well as disagreements with her mother, Lauren decided to participate in a family vacation with her dad to Mexico and then move out on her own. The university she planned on attending had no more openings in the chef's school, but an offer came from her aunt and uncle to live with them and finish year thirteen at Aldergrove Secondary. Taking a wide variety of classes, auto mechanics, peer counseling, dance and acting, she ultimately completed her chef's apprenticeship while living with her Aunt Margaret and Uncle Ed, giving up her horses for a short while.

She graduated from Aldergrove Secondary as a Theory Level One Chef's Apprentice. After spending time cooking in various kitchens and continuing to work with the family horses, Lauren followed a different path incorporating her love of drama and her love of everything equestrian. She decided to focus on the movie business specializing in horses. She wanted to do stunts in movies which would allow her the opportunity to work with horses in the movie industry. Accepted in another apprentice program, she learned about and cared for stunt horses, and she learned special skills necessary for riding horses in films such as *The Pledge* and *The Thirteenth Warrior*. Television shows she performed in were *Nothing Too Good for a Cowboy* and *Dead Man's Gun*. At a movie studio in Mission, B.C., Lauren was in heaven working with over sixty horses. She didn't care if it was raining or the barn was flooding; she was doing what she loved. At this point in her life, she felt that life was great! An agent found her a lot of movie extra work and helped her in getting auditions for bigger parts. At the end of her apprentice program, she was hired on to work at the stunt ranch in Mission.

In June of 2000, Lauren was twenty-two years old and loving life. Taking a break from working full time at the ranch, she and her dog, Cheers, went on a magnificent road trip through the Rocky Mountains from British Columbia to Cockren, Alberta. The goal, visiting a friend during a five day vacation. Lauren felt exhilarated and optimistic about her independent and exciting life, ripe with possibilities. She was living her dream. She could never have imagined what was to come.

Returning to the studio ranch, Lauren got up early the next day to feed the horses as she normally did. Horse chores are always there, vacation or not. One of the older barns that she needed to feed in was actually used in a television series, *Neon Rider,* and this was where her "normal life" changed its course in a very dramatic way. While Lauren was away, other workers had pulled bales from the bottom of the hay stacks leaving a tower of bales tightly wedged between two walls. Lauren climbed up to the top of this tower to throw bales down.

Looking back on this incident, Lauren wonders if she was thinking clearly and maybe should have asked for help. But, as she emphasizes, "I didn't get this job by not getting things done and needing the constant help of others, and I couldn't rationalize having to wake my extremely temperamental boss this early to tell him I couldn't feed the horses because I couldn't get at the hay."

At this point Lauren loosened the top bale of hay so she could throw it down. Realizing that the stack was becoming unsteady, she leapt to the ground. Because she was jumping from a height of approximately ten feet, she crouched as she landed to absorb the shock of hitting the hard ground. Simultaneously as she landed, a bale fell on her back. She was "taken out by a simple bale of hay."

It was instant. Lauren was on the floor with no feeling from her right breast diagonally down to her left hip. Hitting her legs and trying to move them only created a stabbing, breath-taking pain that came from her back. Not being able to take a large enough breath to cry for help, her voice was weak as she cried out. Alone, unable to move and in incredible pain, she lay on the barn floor for what seemed like twenty minutes before someone found her. The help that eventually arrived thought she was being attacked by a horse with little idea what they would find by the hay loft.

As she remembers this day, June 17, 2000, a Saturday, it seemed like the ambulance took forty-five minutes to arrive. While she was being loaded into it, an optimistic Lauren said she would see everyone tomorrow and please remember to feed the buffalo. Her optimism waned as she thought back on body parts she had broken in the past. She knew how good the gas, nitrous oxide, makes you feel so she breathed in as deeply as she could. She was taken to a hospital in Mission. This facility was so small that they closed on weekends except for emergencies, and the nurses were not prepared to handle an emergency such as Lauren's. Lying there, she could hear the nurses and doctor discussing what they should do. One of the nurses thought they should get her out of her hay covered clothing. Cutting Lauren's shirt open, the nurse attempted to slide it out from under her. Lauren compares this movement with someone doing a magic trick and attempting to quickly remove a tablecloth from under a wine glass. Needless to say, this was extremely painful. Her body was jerked to the left and stabbing pain shot threw her back and arms.

She screamed, she cried, and she shouted to the ambulance personnel, "Put me back in the ambulance! Don't leave me here! Take me to Vancouver!" Yelling very loudly now, she made it clear she was not staying in Mission. Back in the ambulance she inhaled another tank of gas and was able to slip into a very teary sleep.

In Vancouver, Lauren awoke to the lurching of the gurney and flashing neon lights and excruciating pain. She was going to now get really good pain killers, but what would kill the emotional pain she was feeling at this time? X-rays were taken and the news of what specific damage had occurred was about to be delivered. But before this, two important people in Lauren's life were there to help her through this. A good friend, Robin Brunei, was the first to arrive and was treated to Lauren flashing her whole nude body. She had forgotten that her clothes had been taken off and was intent on showing him what the nurses did to her jeans and shirt when they cut them. She lifted back the sheets not remembering that her clothing had been removed. He did comment to her later that she had a lovely tan. Good friends say things like that.

Lauren's mother arrived next and was there with Lauren to hear the results of the x-rays. Lauren asked the doctor to please be blunt and not sugar coat anything.

The doctor told her, "It's as bad as it gets. The only way it could be a worse break is if it had been higher up the spine."

She had broken her T11 and her T12 vertebrae were shattered. Her spinal cord had been severed. Only six per cent of people with this type of injury can ever walk again.

Lauren confesses, "A little sugar would have helped that go down."

Who was going to call her dad? Lauren's mom reluctantly agreed she would do it.

Lauren was scheduled for surgery the next day. While she was waiting, she experienced a burning down her body and found out ice exacerbated the fire. She learned that this was neurological pain common after spinal cord injuries. To complicate the situation further, she had extreme pain in her lower abdomen that required many ultra-sounds to diagnose the problem. Because of her pain, an anti-nausea drug was included with her medications. This had the opposite effect than intended and sent her brain into spins. She had not eaten in preparation for the surgery that had been pushed back to the end of the day creating even more discomfort. Adding insult to injury, her surgery was postponed to the next day and then the next day. Because her injury wasn't life threatening and apparently couldn't get worse, she could wait.

Lauren woke up after surgery with one metal bar, three screws and wire mesh wrapped around newly constructed vertebrae created from a bone graft from her hip. She had forty-five stitch strips in her back and many stitches in her hip. She wondered what was next. One thing she knew for certain was her equestrian dreams were shattered as well as her back. She would never ride a horse again.

Chapter 3

Paralyzed from the belly button down, Lauren committed to her decision to never ride again. She was not going to be led around in circles after reaching the levels of success as a horsewoman she had known. That would not be therapeutic for her; in fact, quite the opposite. She did decide to be active, though. To accomplish this, she knew she had to change the negative mind set within and around her.

As she so eloquently told an audience at a Savvy Conference in 2005, "I was being introduced as the girl who **used** to jump the high fences, **used** to ride the tough horses, **used** to do cross country and **used** to work for the movie industry. If I needed to be depressed I could go home and look in the mirror."

To change this mind set, she felt she needed to give people something positive to talk about, and that she did. So why not try tennis, hand cycling, kayaking, downhill mountain biking and sailing? After thirteen days in the hospital and two months at the G.F. Strong Rehabilitation Centre learning to adjust to an unfamiliar existence in a wheelchair, Lauren entered a new phase of her life determined to play the best game she could with the hand she'd been dealt.

Not present at first, this positive attitude took time and healing with help from a variety of therapists; occupational, recreational, vocational and physical, as well as a social worker. One of her therapists was a sex therapist. Six or seven days after her accident, the sex therapist came into her room with a skeleton on wheels. With everything Lauren had to deal with at that time, this seemed a little weird to her. She questioned the therapist wondering if she was teaching her how to give the guy more pleasure since she couldn't feel anything from the hips down. Not surprisingly the therapist did not come back with an answer. It didn't matter anyway at that point. Lauren was at such a low point that she questioned why the doctors didn't cut her legs off. They were just dead weight. In the hospital, Lauren was slapped with more reality when she was put on the ninth floor and the windows were locked shut. Her mother couldn't open them to get her fresh air and was told that suicides were more common on this floor. One nurse denied her the simplest pleasure, putting her flowers in the bathroom where she couldn't enjoy them. But one of the most agonizing experiences was her first visit by her dad. As a child, he had awakened her by rubbing her feet. This was the first thing he did when he found her sleeping in her hospital room. Devastated, both she and her father realized he wouldn't wake her up like this ever again.

The decision that it was time for her to go to rehab resulted from a grueling session with a therapist in the hospital who was trying to teach Lauren to sit up. The therapist left and took a phone call so Lauren attempted to sit up on her own. She did, but couldn't get back down. Terrified she would injure her back further because her stitch strips weren't healed, Lauren was crying for help. The therapist decided, at this point, she was ready for rehab. Lauren did not want to go. She told her mother that they would just teach her how to live in a wheelchair. The taxpayers' money could be better spent on more needy individuals like the homeless because nothing could be done to help her.

But Lauren was wrong. At six weeks post-injury, she was mountain biking on the beautiful, but challenging, Whistler Mountain, shrieking with joy, when she flipped over with the bike attached to her.

People are running to help her and yelling, "Are you okay?"

Lauren, with her wry sense of humor, replies, "I think I broke my back! No, I already did that."

She continues her adventure down the mountain after some assistance, only to see other mountain bikers waving frantically for her to stop. She can't and rides down the trail between a mother bear and her cub. This made for quite a memorable day filled with the exhilaration Lauren needed to move her forward in her rehabilitation process.

Sailing also became a big part of her progress out of despair and back into feeling like a valuable, contributing member of society. Even though she had always been afraid of sharks, she decided they would not be a problem if they bit below the belly button and so she began to sail. One Ronald MacDonald day, she was asked by the Disabled Sailing Association to take a six year old boy out sailing. She said she would, but she felt like the blind leading the blind. She was assured that she could do it! The parents seemed to be horrified watching her dragging her body into the boat. But it was a successful outing with the exception of some throwing up on the boy's part, and became a defining moment in her life. Having always had trouble asking others for help, she discovered she was helping someone else; she had something to offer someone else.

Returning to her mom's house in Aldergrove, Lauren continued to mountain-bike down Whistler Mountain, now made famous by the 2010 Winter Olympics in Vancouver, on a four wheel bike. Sailing had now become a passion that she enjoyed at the Jericho Sailing Center in Vancouver earning her White Sail Level 3 enabling her to sail alone. Solo sailing as a part of the Disabled Sailing Association, she was able to share this love as a volunteer. Taking disabled children out on the water and teaching them to sail was in integral part of her recovery. She knew that despite the paralysis of her legs, she could benefit others. By the end of the summer after her accident, she started racing sail boats and her competitive side resurfaced. She joined the racing team and competed in several regattas. The skills, balance and agility that she had acquired during her early years of riding helped her to adapt to the intricacies of dinghy sailing, which she enjoyed immensely. As a certified dinghy sailor, passing the Canadian Yachting Association White Sail Program Levels 1, 2 and 3, enabled her to become a volunteer sailing instructor. Her achievements through the Disabled Sailing Association earned her a "Volunteer of the Year" award in August of 2001.

Lauren's rehabilitation included dating, and she did have someone special that came into her life at this time who helped her in her rediscovery of life as she would now know it. Perry was a boyfriend and remains a friend. They started out with a rather unusual first date that included a lot of awkwardness and laughing. He showed up at her house and loaded her up in his vehicle. Cramming in her wheelchair, he picked it up by the wheels and they slammed into his shins. Her bag opened and her catheters flew out. Flustered, he didn't know what they were and just hurriedly stuffed everything back in and off they went to play pool. Lauren got stuck under the pool table three times, but when she looked at Perry she just laughed, and he did too. Actually they both considered this a great first date, and it led to an on and off relationship that lasted five years.

Starting out like any new couple, they liked to have fun. Perry and Lauren would "wheel" together, and so he would use her spare chair. Their first Christmas together, they had ordered pizza delivery and then took off for a "wheel". The pizza guy showed up as they were coming up the driveway. He felt so bad that both of them were in wheelchairs he gave them a thirty percent discount. From then on, every time they ordered pizza, Perry would have to get in the chair. Lauren honestly thinks he would have done anything for her, but horses seemed to get in the way.

She did end up riding again, we know that. But how did this come about with her mind set on never climbing up on a horse again? There is a saying in the horse world that when you come off a horse, you get up, dust yourself off and get right back on. Horse people believe if you don't do this, the demons will come and you'll never ride again. Of course, the demons for most riders would be fear and humiliation. Lauren had never known fear around horses, but to get back on a horse after her horrific accident, the demons of embarrassment and depression would be overwhelming. The demon of discouragement was there as well. Losing the freedom and joy she had always felt on a horse's back as well as her competitive edge while striving to be at the top of her game as an equestrian was devastating.

Lauren did however go down to the barn and give lessons to some girls who were riding her horses. While she was at the barn, she was watching one of her old coaches, Sandy Diamond, giving a lunge-line lesson to a young rider, and Lauren broke down in tears. The realization came to her that even though this girl was not a great rider, she could do anything she wanted with a horse. She could get on and off, she could decide to be a pleasure rider, or she could compete in any discipline she wanted. She could do whatever she desired in the equestrian world. Lauren felt, ever so powerfully at that moment, that this choice had been taken away forever. Some uncontrollable external force had stolen her passion and love away from her.

Noticing that Lauren was crying, Sandy emphatically stated, "That's it! You're getting back on a horse!"

Lauren wanted to escape and began wishing she'd paid more attention in wheelchair class about wheeling in the mud. She didn't get far. At this point, two friends picked her up and plopped her up on a horse like a rag doll. She was literally lying on the horse's neck. She had ridden all of her life and at that moment had zero sensation of sitting on a horse. She couldn't feel her legs on the horse and was terrified of falling off. She sat up and started to cry. At this moment, the one thing she had feared most, being led around in circles on a horse, was what was happening to her. One person walked beside her and held her on.

She says, "This was honestly one of the worst experiences of my life and certainly one of the most humiliating. Internally filled with anger, I was taken off the horse and went home to think long and hard about what had just happened and how it would affect my life."

Reflecting back on that moment, Lauren is embarrassed wondering how she could have ever thought she was too good to have to deal with one of life's challenges. This isn't the stuff she is made of. At home that night, Lauren knew she had a major decision ahead of her.

She asked herself, "Was I going to let this gift that had been given me that day go to waste, or was I going to swallow big, dig deep, and get over my feelings of self-pity and humiliation?"

She came to the realization that horses had been taken away from her, for a while, but through some mysterious force, despite her stubborn will, they had been given back to her. Getting up early the next day, Lauren returned to the barn and asked to be put back up on a horse.

Knowing that adaptations were needed in Lauren's tack for her to be able to ride confidently, Lauren and Sandy decided not to try and reinvent the wheel. Sandra Verda, the head of a facility in Langley called the Pacific Riding for the Disabled Association, was a paralympian coach. Sandra had been involved with therapeutic riding and Para- Equestrian sport since 1991. She specializes in coaching those riders who seek independence and competition because it is her love and passion. Ultimately she would shape Lauren's riding, inspire her and support her mentally as she progressed towards becoming a world-class athlete. Lauren called her, and Sandra came over to watch Lauren ride. This visit and Lauren's renewed love of riding led her on an arduous journey consisting of hours of problem solving, adapting saddles, training horses to respond to whip aides, developing special mounting techniques and many more challenges more often than not involving tears. Lauren began seriously training to compete in the Paralympics in dressage. Primarily working with Sandra, Lauren opened a new chapter in her competitive equestrian life. Her dreams would continue, taking a different shape, hopefully leaving the demons behind her.

MOUNTAIN BIKING

Chapter 4

Ralph Waldo Emerson observed that, "Riding a horse is not a gentle hobby, to be picked up and laid down like a game of solitaire, it is a grand passion." Lauren embodies this spirit and passion.

As her coach Sandra Verda explains, "Knowing Lauren, who has gone from tears and never wanting to ride again to aspiring to ride at the most elite level with some of the world's top equestrians with disabilities, has been inspiring."

Lauren exemplifies the power of the mind influencing our experiences whether positive or negative. Sandra, who has become a specialist in coaching paralympians, sees her as the epitome of someone overcoming obstacles with determination, hard work and a positive attitude. She believes Lauren's ability to focus is her greatest strength. Lauren will work at a task determined to keep at it even if it's not going well. Lauren doesn't give up! Assisting her in reaching her Paralympic goal has been her exceptional ability as a rider that she brought with her to the rigorous training needed for dressage competition. Her riding excellence in the past has helped her with her "feel" for the horse, although she has had to learn to use it in a different way.

While training with Sandra Verda and preparing for competition, Lauren began working for the Royal Bank of Canada at a special work station adapted to her wheelchair. But her dream, her long term career goal, was and is success with horses, perhaps becoming the first paralyzed Grand Prix dressage rider and having her own barn, even a ranch where she can raise and train super horses especially for elite, competitive athletes with disabilities She can visualize this and so much more.

Seeing herself as an athlete who just happens to have a disability, reminds Lauren that intensive training to prepare for competitions will have to be a part of her routine. Part of that training includes adaptations to her equipment that she will have to use. Lauren began using Velcro thigh straps, padded knee rolls and elastic bootstraps to keep her legs in place as she rides to allow for a quick breakaway if she begins to fall. In readiness for some hard training, inflatable gel pads were strategically placed on her saddle to protect her tailbone and base of her spine from pressure and percussive sores. Lauren credits Sandra Verda with the accommodations she needs.

These are the equipment modifications. What about balancing and maneuvering a horse? Working with her new skill set, Lauren needs to make accommodations in her riding as well. She must use her abdominal muscles to maintain balance. In controlled movements, instead of the leg pressure she had as an able-bodied rider, she will shift her core weight and use specially adapted riding whips. She is learning to communicate with horses differently.

Lauren's persistence takes her further in her journey towards excellence, and in 2002 she is classified by the International Paralympic Equestrian Committee (IPEC) as a

Grade II rider. This Grade consists of mainly wheelchair users or those with severe locomotor impairment involving the trunk and with good to mild upper limb function, or severe unilateral impairment, according to the Para-Equestrian Classification Rules. Now Lauren is eligible for IPEC competitions and will compete against other riders in her Grade II classification. Serious training for the Paralympics, Para-Equestrian Dressage, specifically, begins.

Para-Equestrian Dressage made its debut in Atlanta in 1996, and has been a part of the Paralympics, the second largest sporting competition in the world, ever since. Often the Paralympics are confused as games for paraplegics. This is not the case. The Paralylmpic Games are held in **parallel** with the Olympic Games. Paralympians are of the highest level of athletic ability representing a variety of disabilities. Para-Equestrians are no exception. Classifications for dressage riders are based on the level of impairment of the athletes, allowing them to be competitive against other athletes with similar disabilities and be judged on their level of skill only. The competition Grade to which these athletes are assigned is based on an assessment by physiotherapists and doctors who evaluate the rider's mobility, strength and coordination. The rider is then given a functional profile number and an identification card issued by the IPEC stating their Grade and listing the approved accommodations the rider can use to compete in their particular grade. Lauren's specific accommodations, as before mentioned, include Velcro straps on her legs, a handlebar on the saddle, bigger knee rolls, elastic bands on her boots, two whips, and the use of voice commands.

Following the Paralympic motto, "Spirit in Motion", Lauren began competing anew not seeing boundaries or limits but limitless possibilities. She had her frustrations but was learning to deal with them and continue towards her goals.

Sandra Verda asked her at this point, "What are your goals?"

Lauren responded, "I want to be able to canter by 2003 and go to the games in Athens."

What if you're not ready?" Sandra asked.

Lauren honestly answered, "It never even crossed my mind"

This moment was an epiphany for Lauren and impressed Sandra Verda resulting in 2002 proving to be a very exciting and productive year for Lauren with competitions in Europe, Canada, and the United States. The Inner Vision Championships in New York where she was awarded the Grade II Individual championship bringing home three gold medals was the highlight. After New York, Lauren was hooked. She knew she was in it for the long haul.

She remembers, "… being on such a high, excited and running on adrenalin. I've been wishing for a long time that I could have that feeling back."

With successes in Portugal, sixth out of twenty-one riders and locally, at the Langley Regional Championships, receiving the high score of seventy-five per cent making her the Grade II Winner, Lauren was on her way believing in her ability not her disability. But unlike the high of New York's Inner Vision Championships, her trip to Portugal was, without any doubt, a test of this belief.

Chapter 5

As we go through our lives, painful and tragic events can overwhelm us and force us to ask if it's possible to endure anything more. "Why is this happening to me?" is a question often asked, and Lauren is not the exception. Her experiences in Portugal at the European Dressage Championships for Riders with Disabilities certainly tested her perseverance and faith in her ability to overcome adversity.

This is her first trip "across the water" since her accident, September, 2002. She is sixteen months post-injury and anxious to find out how she will stand up to other world class Para-Equestrian riders, as is her Canadian Team. She is traveling with the team, the team manager and support staff. Lauren enjoys her trip from Vancouver to Toronto, only to find out, upon arrival there, that her whips have not arrived. Lost somewhere? She has no idea. But she does meet up with the rest of her team, three riders from Eastern Canada. They fly together to Portugal via Spain landing in Lisbon. Arriving without her luggage as well as losing her whips, Lauren is beginning to view this trip as more of a challenge than she expected. No luggage means no replacement for her indwelling catheter she uses to fly. With this she doesn't have to find a restroom on a plane or worry about becoming dehydrated. She can drink the amount she wants and empty the catheter into a bottle as necessary. This probably sounds fairly simple except for the fact that her body does not adapt to the catheter, and if left in for two days or longer she develops a bladder infection. Her body is fighting the foreign object within it. Without her bags she can't take the catheter out and she is wearing the same clothes. Three days later, feeling ill, Lauren tells her team that if her bags do not arrive by the next day she will have to return to Canada. The team has the idea of driving by a local hospital to see if they have medical supplies she could use. She needs her intermittent catheters. After seeing the condition of the hospital, Lauren decides she will take her chances with the situation as it is. On the evening of the fourth day of their arrival in Portugal, Lauren's baggage finally appears.

"I can tell you I never wore the clothing I had worn for four days again. I think I may have burned them!" she explained during a retelling of this experience.

But this is only the beginning of a journey fraught with complications. Unfortunately a common problem for Para-Equestrians is that they are not riding horses of their own. The team will be borrowing horses from the Portuguese Army, and it is necessary to try them to determine if they have any talent at dressage, and if they will match up with their riders. One is selected for Lauren that has been given a year off because he flipped over a jump and suffered paralysis on the right side of his neck.

At this point Lauren mentions, "How fitting!"

The horse, damaged but resilient, trains with Lauren for six days in pouring rain, day after day. The only upside to the rain is the fragrant smell of the eucalyptus that fills the air after it stops. And then it is off from Lisbon to Porto for the competition.

Arriving at the competition grounds, it is so wet and sloppy Lauren can't even wheel. She is parked under a tree to wait or put in a wheelbarrow to be pushed. The stables are flooded. There is no point in grooming the horses because they are just covered in mud and clay within minutes. Despite these adverse circumstances, Lauren does well. Placing fifth and sixth against top riders, she is thrilled! Some reward for all she has endured up to this point including a bed so hard she thinks she is actually sleeping on a box spring and a ramp into her sleeping area that is so steep she can't get up it on her own.

Could this trip get any worse? Oh yes! Her flight home is when things really fell apart. As in her trip over, she has to fly from Portugal to Spain before heading back to Canada. Waiting for her chair on the airplane in Spain for what seems like hours, the frantic attendants keep bringing Lauren one awful broken down old chair after another trying to convince her that this is hers.

They ask, "Are you sure this is not your chair?"

She replies, as only Lauren can, "You'd think I'd know what my legs look like!"

Her chair isn't found, so she is pushed in another chair as fast as possible to catch the connecting flight. Not speaking any English, the man racing her through the airport is totally panicked, and Lauren, feeling like she is in a race, bumping into people and things, has admitted enjoying this a little. She actually starts laughing even though she is upset about the loss of her chair.

Upon arriving at the check-in gate, the team finds out that the stand-by passengers have boarded. Lauren and the rest of the team are so late that their seats have been given away. With only four seats left on board and four athletes and four support staff, the decision is made to send the four disabled people home alone. The plane is so far out on the tarmac, the team has to take a shuttle out to it, and the driver can't find the plane. The driver keeps repeating, "No problemo." But as far as Lauren is concerned it is a problem for her. No wheelchair, no assistant and a missing plane! Half an hour later, the plane is located and Lauren finds herself being rapidly wheeled out across the tarmac and into a large hose. Seeing what is coming, she yelps as the front wheels of the chair come to a sudden stop.

She becomes airborne landing on the hard tarmac as the man pushing her looks at her and says, "Oh, no walkie?"

Losing it at this point, Lauren tearfully shrieks, "Yes, I am sitting in a crumpled mess on the tarmac in front of a plane full of people because I can walk!"

Now on the plane and in tears because she has strained her wrist falling, she has had enough! Seeing her crying the flight attendant feels so bad for her that she offers her a drink. Taking advantage of this, Lauren orders a much deserved double. After downing her drink, she begins to smell something funny, kind of like burnt popcorn. Burning anything is not what you want to smell on an airplane. She looks down at her leg and discovers that the tubing to her indwelling catheter has become disconnected from her leg bag in the fall. She has peed all down her leg. She is soaked and with no assistant!

All the way back to Toronto, Lauren has the time to think about "Why me?" "Why is this happening to me?" She wonders does she really need this. Answering her own questions, she remembers back to the hospital during her recovery when she made the decision to be a survivor of the things life throws at us. She knew if she wanted to be successful, she would have to determine what attitude would help her achieve greatness. At that point she changed the "Why me?" to "Why not me?" These sorts of things happen to others, why not me? She also figured out at that time that this attitude works with all the wonderful things in life.

Instead of saying to herself, "I'll never be able to ride as good as anyone else." She decided at that moment in time to say, "Why not? Why not me? Why can't I win gold? Why not me!"

Lauren and her chair reunite in Toronto. It doesn't look exactly like she remembered it. It is more wobbly and bent, nevertheless like her it has endured. Yes, Lauren placed well in the Portuguese competition, but the life changing accomplishment in Portugal is the answer to why me?

Chapter 6

Lauren returns from Portugal with new found wisdom and renewed purpose towards fulfilling her goals. In May of 2003, Lauren accompanied by Sandra Verda, travels to Germany to train at the International Academy for Equestrian Studies in Warendorf. They are privileged to ride numerous dressage schoolmasters, older, well-mannered, upper-level dressage horses, and train with coaches for the German Paralympic Equestrian team. These sessions are productive and Lauren is able to work on some advanced movements such as canter, half pass and flying changes, a tremendous accomplishment. Riding several different horses, Sandra notes Lauren's exemplary ability to adapt to each horse and perform under pressure. Lauren is poised for success! She comes home to find herself ranked the number one Grade Two Paralympic rider in Canada in international competition.

Keeping the momentum going, Lauren finds herself in Belgium at the Individual World Championships placing sixth, seventh and eighth out of thirty-six riders. This is a tough competition that starts on an outstanding lease horse

Lauren had arranged for ahead of time named Charlie Brown and ends with a dramatic change of mounts. Charlie Brown appears to have a funny hitch in his front leg. Lauren's coach doesn't think he will pass the vet check so two days before the competition they find her a small, white horse named Prada. She is very strong and pulls on Lauren's arms and hands a lot. She has a great go, but Lauren feels like she is being dragged around the dressage ring. Although discouraged because she thought she had a wonderful horse to ride and because this was the next stepping stone to Athens, she decides to focus on what she needs to make it there. What will she need to do to survive another day and accomplish her long term goal? She is successful in this endeavor, but in keeping with her now international travel tradition, Lauren loses her video and camera in one of the taxis on the way home. The good news is the Paralympic Games in Athens are coming in 2004, and Lauren is officially qualified to ride for Team Canada.

With this success comes heartache. The stress of training for the Athens Games has put a severe strain on Lauren's relationship with Perry. She is not able to put the effort needed into it, and she is tired of arguing about his perception that he is last in her priorities. Lauren breaks up with him over dinner at a public restaurant. Later she is to regret the way she handled their break up , nevertheless she moves on to date someone else. Her new boyfriend lives out of town, and a weekend relationship seems easier to handle after her experiences with Perry. Perry, although unhappy with this new situation, still buys Lauren a new dressage riding jacket, shirt and gloves before her trip to Athens. As hurt as he is, he still supports Lauren in every way he can. After Athens, Lauren and Perry try living together and Lauren really wants to commit to a functional relationship. But instead of doing things together, Lauren's life has become all about training and competing, getting ready for Beijing, 2008. She makes

Perry attend a horse event that she needs to be at on his birthday. She realizes that he stood by her, and she's not really sure what he got in return. Lauren ends up breaking up with Perry again, but they will still remain friends, talking regularly on the phone. Lauren has to move on and follow the course she has begun.

In early 2004 Lauren is nominated by the Paralympic Selection Committee for the Canadian Team and then officially named to the team. Other accolades include her win of the Freestyle High Score at the Amherst Dressage Show and her rank as the number one Para-Equestrian Rider in Canada. Lauren is awarded the Equine Canada George Jacobson Equestrian of the Year Award during 2004 based on her accomplishments for that year which include finishing seventh in her Championship Test and sixth in her Freestyle Test at the Markopoulo Equestrian Center in the Athens Games. Her mount for the Athens games is Dior, a fifteen year old gelding that had been a top international dressage horse in the 1990's owned by Andrea Taylor who would later become the national coach for the Canadian Para-Equestrian Team. Were it not for difficulty executing a perfect halt, bringing the horse to a complete stop on command, during competition, Lauren would have been on the podium. Unfortunately, Dior wants to piaffe, or dance in place, and Lauren does not have the physical use of her legs to push him into compliance. She just can't get him to halt. This problem will happen twice denying her a medal.

Lauren sighs when thinking about those games, "We went from mellow and safe to here we are in Athens and we needed to take that chance and hit it. I had amazing marks with some of the judges giving me second place marks, but I could not get Dior to halt. With judges' comments like, 'Such a spectacular ride! Your horse and you go so well together, a pity about the halt," Lauren continues, "that can make you cry."

Had Lauren gotten a score of six in the halt, she would have been wearing Athens silver and bronze. It was that close.

Lauren, with her indomitable spirit and positive attitude, sums the experience up like this, "The thought that I qualified for Athens in two years was remarkable to me because I had such a short time to train, and the thing with dressage is its preciseness. I only had a short time to put together a whole test, and couldn't go back and make every part perfect. I had to keep moving on. I had to keep learning new stuff so I could at least come to the arena with something."

In Athens, Lauren competes against twenty of the world's elite Paralympic dressage riders in her grade, with the top ten having over fifteen years experience in top-level competition. Lauren has two. What she doesn't have in years of experience she has in a cheering section. Four of her aunts and uncles and her mom and dad are there to support her. Lauren wonders if it is the excitement of the competition, her first Paralympic Games with family watching her, or possibly just old-fashioned nerves bringing out an expanded sensitivity in Dior. But the halt just doesn't come.

After Athens, Lauren experiences a huge let down, a depression that leaves her crying a lot. Dior stayed in Belgium with her coach, Sandra Verda, for about two months and so Lauren doesn't do much riding. Her life feels upside down. She has given up so much of her social life to achieve making it to Athens, and now people don't call. She has turned down too many invitations too many times. Everyone assumes she will say no. She goes from an incredible high only to be met by a dramatic low. Lauren realizes this is something commonly experienced among top athletes who are totally focused on a goal, make it and then ask, "Now what?"

But Lauren uses this experience to regroup. Already preparations for her overarching goal of Beijing 2008 are being formulated. The next big event is The Open European

Championships for Disabled Riders in Soskut, Hungary, July 26th through the 31st, 2005. Again Lauren is the only rider in the competition who is on a borrowed horse. Despite this, she scores a 74.55 percent in Grade II Dressage, to finish in fourth place, just .11 per cent away from the bronze medal.

"I was very happy with my result," remarks Lauren, "especially since I was competing against the top riders in my sport. To be able to achieve this score gives me great confidence for a medal in the future."

Sandra Verda elaborates more, "It was definitely a challenging two weeks with only six days of training on our borrowed horse and with extremely hot temperatures. Lauren coped well and rose to the occasion producing some very respectable scores against tough competition."

Competing not only in Paraequestrian events, Lauren has competed against able-bodied riders starting in 2004. This has not only been an education for her, but for the competitors and judges in the able-bodied dressage world as well. Her first able-bodied show was at the Thunderbird Equestrian Center on Dior. She was entered in first and second level classes. Lauren had her dispensation card with her stating the adaptations to her tack and that she could use her voice and only salute with her head. The FEI (Federation Equestrian International) has determined that these compensating aids put her on a level playing field with other riders. She had a fantastic second level test performing a counter canter, travers, shoulders in, walk pirouettes and ten meter canter circles. Lauren won the class.

Two ladies in her line looking at scores were commenting, as Lauren remembers, something like this, "Well of course she won the class! She was riding Dior, a retired Grand Prix horse trained by Andrea Taylor."

Lauren is thinking to herself that Dior is not an easy horse to ride. She wanted to say, "I'll trade you. You ride Dior without your legs or lower core, and I'll ride your horse with the use of legs."

It seemed funny to Lauren at the time that it didn't even cross their minds that she was paralyzed.

At Southlands, Lauren had an even more extreme experience. At that time competitions were still new to Para Classes. When Lauren went to check in at administration, the woman at the registration looked around and asked, "Who is judging the disabled dressage class?"

Lauren replied, "The dressage is actually fine, not disabled at all."

Later in the day, when the upper level dressage judge saw Lauren trotting down the center line, she blew her whistle and called Lauren's coach over to her. "I can't judge this rider. She's tied on a horse. It would violate my insurance."

Explaining that under FEI rules, Lauren could not be tied on and that all the Velcro straps would break free if anything happened; the judge was satisfied. At the end of the day this judge came over to Lauren and had a wonderful conversation with her and was extremely impressed.

Lauren had quite an emotional test in a competition in West Palm Beach. People there were very uptight about Lauren and her wheelchair in part because her power chair scared their high class horses.

At the wash rack, not seeing Lauren, one woman commented, "There is a place for people like her. It's called the Special Olympics!"

This really offended Lauren for two reasons. One, the woman was not educated enough to know the difference between a Para Rider and a Special "O" Rider. Two, this woman didn't know who Lauren was and what she was capable of. There is some educating to do, and Lauren has been and will continue to be a part of that.

In contrast, Lauren has encountered judges who have called her over when she rode into the ring and asked what class she was riding, that they had a Para class listed as next. After seeing her ride, they thought she was an able-bodied rider. Lauren considers this a fantastic compliment!

Her grooms share the wonderful comments people make after she has gone by. "She is a Paralympian, and she rides better than most able bodied riders. She is so inspirational."

These comments outweigh the ignorance and make Lauren feel really good! Lauren has ridden in approximately twenty-five able-bodied classes and usually places in the top three. She is making a difference for all Para-Athletes.

Exhibiting phenomenal strength of character is what Lauren is all about, and she takes this to others as a motivational speaker on topics such as: the pursuit of excellence, being innovative to succeed, setting goals, team work and overcoming adversity. She knows of what she speaks. She is involved with the Rick Hansen "Wheels in Motion Foundation" as a committee volunteer and as an ambassador. She speaks eloquently about the challenges of spinal cord injury as does her personal coach Sandra Verda.

"She is proof that people with disabilities play a key role in our society, and they are able to adapt themselves to meet their new environment, thus allowing them to lead full and productive lifestyles. Furthermore," Sandra asserts, "she is a testimony to everyone, that achieving your dreams is possible."

Achieving your dreams is possible, but not always easy. Not only have the elusive medals Lauren passionately wants been just beyond her grasp, but she is headed towards Beijing with an overwhelming feeling of not being sure what she really wants out of life. "What's next?" she asks. She doesn't want to work in the bank forever. After going to the Paralympics in Athens, devoting four years of her life to preparation for this event, the build-up is huge, the let down even greater. This leaves a big hole in her life along with the disappointment that with Dior, owned by Andrea Taylor and leased to Sandra Verda, she does not feel she has a true partner. This being another obstacle to overcome in addition to some questions she is asking herself about dressage competition, questions that are leaving her burnt out and unmotivated to compete. These qualities are not in her nature and she needs answers. They will come and in a very unexpected, but exciting way. Answers that will make a sea change in her life.

LAUREN RIDING DIOR

Chapter 7

Synchronicity, the mysterious convergence of events, can be a powerful force for change if a person is open and willing to take a leap of faith. Lauren was ready. True synchronicity implies that these events are unlikely to occur together by chance, and unlikely as it was, serendipity appeared in Lauren's life. Her name was Shannon Hendrickson and her step-father knew Pat Parelli.

Shannon's husband, Rusty, had come into the bank where Lauren worked in Aldergrove and was in her line. He had seen Lauren in the local paper and asked her how her riding was going. They chatted about the fact that his kids were going to do their Level 1 test in Parelli Natural Horsemanship in Vernon, a town about four and a half hours away. Lauren mentioned that she was familiar with PNH and had done Level 1 herself with her Hungarian mare. A few days later, Shannon called Lauren and shared that the Love, Language and Leadership Tour would be in Vernon in May. Her step-father, Larry Stewart, a Four Star Parelli instructor, and her mother Lesley, owned Parelli Natural Horsemanship, Canada. He could introduce Lauren to Pat and Linda Parelli. Shannon continued to explain that her real father was paralyzed from the waist down and had taught her how to ride. She wanted to help Lauren. She offered to drive Lauren to meet the Parellis if Lauren could drive to her house. Lauren had never met Shannon, she had no idea where this opportunity would lead, but she took the leap of faith four weeks later and drove to Shannon's house.

PEANUT AND LAUREN

Lauren was actually very familiar with Parelli Natural Horsemanship. A trainer, Sandy Diamond, had sparked Lauren's interest in this program in 1994 when Lauren was having difficulties with her Hungarian mare, Cayenne, aka Peanut. Her mare was extremely exuberant, highly sensitive as well as quick and smart, quicker and smarter than Lauren. This left Lauren extremely frustrated, but what she experienced earlier with the Parelli program was one of those synchronic pieces in her life that would be an integral part of her equestrian future. Lauren just didn't know it at the time. Because the program is focused on developing a partnership between horse and human without force, it develops love, language and leadership leading to success for both partners. With the help of the Seven Games, assisting humans to partner with horses through fun while improving communication and leadership, Peanut progressed from not being able to stand still and leaping in the air, to being hooked on Lauren. Lauren could ride her bareback and bridleless while jumping fences. She found the lightness, fun and safety that she needed with this mare. She and Peanut developed an enviable relationship that continued after Lauren's accident.

One sad, gloomy visit home post-injury, Lauren was staring off into the field and to her surprise Peanut came trotting towards her. She stood at the gate calling for her. When Lauren wheeled over to her, Peanut dropped her head into Lauren's lap letting her know she missed her. They sat for some time, with Peanut never leaving Lauren's side. All of this gave Lauren the courage to take the next step and halter the mare. Lauren played all seven Parelli games with her from her wheelchair. Lauren effortlessly loaded her into a horse trailer and saw that Peanut looked at her eager to do more. For Lauren, accomplishing more turned into challenging her newfound transportation. The next ten minutes of her life were a true test of trust as Lauren let the horse pull her like a chariot down the road. Lauren knew at that moment horses would still be a part of her life. Peanut became one of the few horses Lauren could handle on the ground from her wheelchair. Tucking this information away "in a storage closet", as she puts it, she had no idea the impact it would later have on her life.

Back at the tour stop, Shannon introduces Lauren to Pat and Linda Parellli. Lauren sees a cowboy with a huge mustache wearing jeans, boots and a cowboy hat with his lovely Australian born wife Linda, an excellent horsewoman and teacher in her own right. Lauren will come to know Pat's humor, energy and passionate love for horses and his ability to change horse and human lives with his showmanship style and a concrete program based on education and experience. Lauren, remembering how effective the "natural way" was with Peanut, boldly shared her dreams and goals to be the first paralyzed rider to ride Grand Prix and to compete in Beijing at the 2008 summer Paralympics with Pat and Linda. Lauren wanted gold, but not just using traditional dressage methods that were sometimes harsh or forced. She felt there had to be an easier way.

Pat describes their first meeting like this, "I remember meeting Lauren and thinking this girl can accomplish anything she puts her mind to. She truly embodies what the Parelli method stands for, inspiration, empowerment and making the world a better place for horses and humans."

"Meeting Pat and learning his method transformed me; I became more emotionally and mentally fit," says Lauren. "I realized there was so much to learn, about myself and my relationship with my horse. When I started studying Parelli everything just clicked."

The result of this meeting was an invitation from Pat for Lauren to come to Colorado for two weeks, and he would see if he felt he could help her to fulfill her dreams. The weekend of this first meeting turned out to be overwhelming for Lauren. With the organization of Leslie Stewart of PNH Canada and Pat's enthusiasm for helping others, the audience made donations for Okanogan Therapeutic Riding and Lauren. Raising ten thousand dollars, Lauren was shocked. It had taken her months of planning an event to raise half of what was done in one hour. Before coming to Colorado, though, Lauren had some homework to do. Pat Parelli has given the horse world a natural and progressive program through developing levels of learning to create harmonious partnerships with horses and their humans respecting the dignity of the horse. Lauren prepares herself by refreshing her Level 1 and starting work on Levels 2 and 3. Now she is motivated. She describes it as a "fire lit under her butt." She is learning and playing with her mare, Peanut, and finds that this is the highlight of her day. Jonathon Field, a local Parelli Instructor, comes to her barn to help her so she would be ready to work with Pat. Lauren is not going to let this opportunity slip through her hands. By August 27, 2005, Lauren and her now good friend Shannon are on a plane heading to Colorado.

SHANNON AND LAUREN

Chapter 8

If driving to Shannon's house is a leap of faith, how can this trip to Colorado best be described? Lauren calls it a summer of firsts, some huge firsts. These firsts require trust, ability, overwhelming courage and sometimes a sense of humor. Right at her side with a huge helping of support, is Pat Parelli. He knows Lauren is paralyzed from the belly button down but not paralyzed in spirit. He helps her prove this to herself. Significant riding breakthroughs are certainly a part of this summer of firsts, but being abandoned in her cabin with a bat and no light makes quite an impression on Lauren as well.

Shannon stays with Lauren the first week and like any true friend who detests bugs, she debugs their cabin with super toxic bug spray. Night after night she bombs their room with Lauren hiding in her sleeping bag. The room becomes a cloud of toxic spray. Nevertheless Shannon will not be satisfied until all the bugs are eliminated. Lauren is just relieved she isn't eliminated too. After one week with Lauren in Colorado, Shannon flies home to attend her son's first day of kindergarten leaving Lauren with a bug free if not bat free cabin.

One evening after Shannon's departure, two women from the ranch come up to Lauren's cabin with her to help her settle in. They help Lauren get in bed and while organizing a few things accidentally move her wheelchair out of her reach.

One of the women keeps repeating, "Wow, that's a big bug!"

Lauren, knowing all the bugs had been killed, looks up, realizes what she is seeing and says, "That is not a bug; it's a bat!"

The room clears, and the women, taking the lantern, leave Lauren alone. Finally they realize that Lauren can't get to her wheelchair and come back to help her and chase out the bat. With no electricity or bathroom in her little cabin, but lots of wildlife, Lauren has some brand new challenges to face.

Another bizarre episode from this trip to Colorado is Shannon plugging in the battery to Lauren's scooter in the wrong place. She fries the "mother board" leaving Lauren without her scooter. Lauren is actually riding a horse when she smells smoke and turns around to watch it burn. So the solution to finding transportation for Lauren is, of course on the Parelli Ranch, a golf cart with the roof taken off. This way she can haul around a wheel chair and play with horses from the ground as well. This appears to be a great idea until Lauren forgets to unplug the power cord as she takes off one day down a mountain driving the golf cart with a stick on the accelerator. When she hears a thumpty-thump, she knows she has a problem. But she laughs about these stories now. They are all part of her summer of firsts.

The first day of riding, Lauren's first horse to play with is Pat's son Caton's stallion named Liberty Major. Sitting on him her first evening there, Lauren is nervous, terrified really of doing something wrong, and riding in front of Pat for the first time. But, living up to his name, Liberty gives Lauren an exhilarating sense of freedom and confidence doing flying lead changes and spins while Lauren grins ear to ear. Despite her fears, her first day of firsts is an overall success!

Day two, Lauren is playing at liberty with Liberty in the round corral. (Liberty work is maneuvers or games done with no halter or lead line from the ground.) After this first, the biggest first of all is still to come. Pat tells Lauren she and Liberty will be helping him to move cows! Not only has Lauren not been outside an arena since her accident, but she doesn't know what to do with cows. Fear and excitement are screaming for dominance inside her brain. Her wild spirit says let's go for it and her brain logically battles back with questions like is she sure she can do this? Lauren takes a deep breath, tries to hide away this myriad of feelings and just enjoy the day. The sun is on her face, she is in the beautiful Colorado Rocky Mountains, the air is fresh and the fields are green. She knows Pat wouldn't ask her to do something she isn't capable of. Pat also reassures her that his cows are smart!

As Lauren rides down through the bunch of them, she remembers telling Liberty, "I have no idea what I'm doing and I need you to help out. Actually I wouldn't be offended at all if you would just take the lead, and I would gladly be a wonderfully grateful passenger."

Two hours later, Lauren has moved cows and ridden through the mountains with Pat and Caton. Lauren explains that, "I just wanted to scream out. I wanted to scream out thank you. I wanted to try and explain what I was feeling and words escaped me for the whole journey."

Up and down steep hills, through trails, Pat asks her, "Are you okay?"

All Lauren can utter is, "This is awesome, awesome!" Inside she is thinking, "This is way beyond awesome; this is true freedom!"

This range of emotions from extreme exhilaration to abject fear characterizes Lauren's earliest Colorado experiences with Pat at the ranch. Lauren articulates these feelings passionately, "Frankly, I was afraid and at the same time wanted more. You see when you have finally come to terms with the loss of something very important to you, it is hard to imagine and try to dream of anything else." Lauren had freedom; she had the use of her legs for twenty-two years along with the ability to be an active participant in arduous outdoor activities. She continues, "As hard as it was, I believe I graciously came to terms with the loss of everything that was dear to me: cross country running, jumping horses, diving, mountain biking and being free with my horse as I galloped through mountains, through water and along spectacular trails. I remember well, with tears in my eyes, saying good-bye to the life I had known and hello to a life I would not have chosen for anyone, not even my worst enemy. I halfheartedly smiled at my new life with a timid eagerness to overcome the challenges ahead, not ever wanting to look back as it would be too painful. With a flight to Colorado, I was now faced fully with one of the true passions of my past. "

In the shower the night after her ride in the mountains with Pat and his cows, Lauren feels a healing release of tears of pain, anger, frustration and mostly the passion for what she feels the future now holds for her. She asks herself, "Do I dare dream?"

Sometimes dreams require a little magic though. So Magic manifests itself, this summer of firsts, in the form of a black quarter horse mare. Now this isn't just any mare. This is Pat Parelli's beautiful black mare from Tasmania, nicknamed the Tasmanian Devil. Not anymore. With Pat she has been transformed, and this very special horse puts her heart and soul in Lauren's hands. Lauren is going to ride her and feel another gift of freedom. Within a week, Lauren is doing flying changes down a straight line on a horse without the use of her legs, then doing a piaffe on the spot and spinning in circles rapidly without falling off! Was this magic? Lauren says no! This is the result of an effective way of playing with and riding a horse and a very special horse named Magic. Lauren feels she has to be special to put the trust in her that she did. Riding a horse for the first time, normally Lauren has to adapt to it and just try to survive in order to accomplish anything close to her goal in a very short time. This is not the case with Magic, a truly exceptional horse.

While playing with Magic from her wheelchair, Lauren knows that Magic's interest in her is beyond fear of something different. Magic confirms this when Lauren's wheelchair breaks and Lauren has to fix her wheels. Lauren has noticed, in the past, two very different reactions from horses under these circumstances. One can be the horse completely ignoring her, while she is flipping over her chair and trying to fix a wheel with a wrench, hammer, screwdriver and spray bottle while holding on to her horse. The other more extreme reaction is for the horse to snort and run away. Magic takes complete interest in what Lauren is doing. She wants to get right in there and help Lauren with her muzzle. It is as if Magic is trying to understand what Lauren is doing and why. The real test of this new relationship will come in a few days at the Savvy Conference, 2005, riding in front of two thousand people.

My first introduction to Lauren is at this conference. I am new to Parelli, Savvy Conferences, Colorado and the incredible energy and love that is generated at these events in this most scenic and yes, spiritual of venues, Pagosa Springs. With a view of the magnificent Pagosa Peak from the arena where the performances take place to the lush fields and statuesque aspens and pines, this is the perfect setting for transformative experiences. I had no idea how perfect! Lauren is introduced by Pat on our last day, a Sunday, with a short recapping of her story up to this point and sharing of her goals to go to the 2008 Paralympics in Beijing as well as riding able bodied in Grand Prix Dressage. He mentions Lauren's struggles in riding borrowed horses that were heavy and hard to ride without legs. Lauren needs to find lightness. Traditional riding methods are not working for her. Pat has invited her down to the ranch to see if he can help her. He knows the audience will be amazed by what they are about to see.

Then Lauren arrives in the arena being pushed in her wheelchair by no less than Pat himself making her chair do wheelies. He jokes that Lauren already has him trained. There is a round corral set up and the crew brings in a golf cart that Lauren can use to play with Magic on the ground. All of us in the audience watch Lauren and Magic play as Pat steps aside to give them center stage. We see a confident, beautiful and poised young woman totally in tune with this magical horse. Moving in harmony to music, she has the audience mesmerized. Magic is bridleless, trotting and cantering beside Lauren's cart with her, circling at the slightest suggestion and jumping barrels with exuberance. Lauren's face exudes a calm, gentle focus that elicits a quiet and willing responsiveness from Magic. Lauren lovingly strokes Magic's face as the audience sits awed and silent except when the silence is broken by enthusiastic applause. But there is more to come. As Magic canters in a circle around Lauren, the round corral panels are moved to open the whole arena. At this point, Magic comes up to Lauren's cart and puts her head in to be bridled. Lauren's beautiful smile performing this task radiates the gratitude she is feeling for this unique and wonderful horse.

Lauren describes this moment like this, "When it was time to bridle Magic, I looked into her eyes and felt her soft hair against my skin, her breathing against my chest, and she put her head in my lap. I knew then everything would turn out great."

To comprehend this last comment, it's important to understand that this young woman who appears so confident and poised is actually terrified of appearing at a Savvy Conference in front of this huge audience, let alone playing with and riding a horse who is a favorite with Parelli folks world-wide. Finding out later how close Lauren came to not coming out is amazing because that is so different from how she appeared. She describes her heart rushing fast that day and a terrible pounding in her ears. Once she has been pushed out into the arena, there is no turning back. Still nervous while playing with Magic, she becomes calm when the mare puts her head in her lap.

After bridling Magic, Lauren is then assisted up into her special saddle by Pat and Caton. She is strapped on to the horse, Pat and Caton check and re-check every part of the saddle, Lauren puts on her helmet and is handed her sticks. Stepping out to an incredibly smooth and exhilarating ride, she is enthusiastically and emotionally received by her audience. Tears of joy and amazement are rolling down cheeks not just of women, but some tough cowboys in the audience. She is performing half-passes, cantering with fluidity and then doing flying changes, concluding with the piaffe and spins. The audience is on their feet, they are going wild, Linda Parelli is looking down from the sound booth clapping and glowing with pride, and these people know they have just witnessed something so special. They have been touched. She touches my heart.

Wondering how this could get any better the audience sees Pat hand Lauren a microphone. She is going to share the long and challenging journey that brought her here. As she tells her story of her accident and re-entry back into the world of horses, her passion to motivate and inspire people is evident. She tells a funny story about a conversation she had with Pat while she was watching people working on the ranch, feeding, shoveling manure and doing all the chores that are required on a working ranch.

She regretfully lamented, "I feel as useless as tits on a bull. I wish I could help."

Pat responded, "Just be the best person you can be and motivate others to greatness against great odds."

In her talk, Lauren aspires to that goal, and perhaps surpasses it. She enthusiastically relates the stories of her two weeks of firsts. In particular, she shares the joy but also the dread of playing with Smart Seven, precious, precious, Smart Seven. This is a youngster that the whole Parelli world has watched being trained by Pat on DVD's. So the pressure is really on. Nevertheless playing with Smart Seven is as successful as all her other firsts reinforcing her concluding statement that with the right attitude and the right tools anything is possible. Pat rides out on another horse, Cash, and asks the audience if it's possible to help her achieve her goal of going to the 2008 Paralympics in Beijing. The audience roars. Collecting from the Parelli Community starts that very day.

Describing her ride on Magic, with so little and such lightness, Lauren comments that she had known this was out there. Now she has found it in Magic and with Parelli Natural Horsemanship. She will no longer be introduced as the girl who **used** to ride the toughest horses and jump the highest fences. She will now be introduced as the Canadian Equestrian of the Year. She and Pat exchange a warm hug on horseback and the audience sits down knowing that each and every one of us has been profoundly touched.

During the break following her performance, Lauren learns a lot from people's responses. She realizes why she is riding for these people. It is not techniques or how to ride that she is teaching them; it is that she **is** riding. She has taught them what someone is capable of doing with so little, and they learn something about themselves.

Lauren says, "I often forget this when I ride. I fail to remember what I shouldn't be able to do and only think about what I want to do and what I am going to work towards doing. Sometimes this makes me have attitude challenges because I forget my disability and I think I should be able to do it all, be able to do what everyone around me is doing. I get frustrated especially on a horse when I am not able to do something right away or the way others do."

Lauren sums up her summer of firsts like this, "Pat and his horses have helped me to discover what I am capable of. With their continued help, I know I will achieve greatness."

This prophetic comment foreshadows a future filled with, yes, greatness but even more grueling challenges ahead.

MAGIC HELPING LAUREN

Chapter 9

Lauren returns to Canada with an invigorated mental and physical fitness. She knows deep down inside her that her dream of making it to Beijing, 2008, is accomplishable. She wants to have a true partnership with her horse using all the four savvies taught in Parelli Natural Horsemanship. Now she has the tools with which to succeed in competition. She is especially honored and thrilled at an invitation coming at the end of her summer of firsts, to attend a dressage clinic with Pat and Linda Parelli and the great master, Walter Zettl. Lauren's friends at Parelli Canada support her by sponsoring her flight to Texas where the clinic is to take place. She will be staying with friends of the Parelli's, Bill and Susan Casner. As a bonus, she will also get to meet Michael Richardson, an amazing rider who is also paralyzed from the waist down. An opportunity for a demo ride at the clinic is planned for Lauren with her old friend and partner, Magic.

One interesting aspect of the clinic for Lauren, besides the benefit of working with Pat again, is going to be the bringing together of different riding disciplines to work as one. This is fascinating to Lauren because she believes, and it is so true, that each discipline has a lot to offer and yet, is similar in many ways. Pat and Linda's horses wow the crowd, and Lauren's demonstration ride on Magic is spectacular. She makes her performance immediately relevant performing movements people are learning in the clinic.

Staying with the Casners and enjoying their phenomenal hospitality is a highlight of her trip. Not only have they built an amazing house and barn on their beautiful property, but the room Lauren stays in makes her feel like a princess. The bed is huge and high, making it difficult for her to get off and on it, but she isn't going to decline this chance of living in luxury for three days and nights. The bathroom comes complete with a Jacuzzi tub that helps her master getting off and on the bed and will certainly make her trip memorable. It seems to be possessed.

One evening while Lauren is relaxing in a bubble bath, she turns the Jacuzzi jets on in the tub. She enjoys this experience for a while and then decides to turn them off and get out. After ten minutes of attempting to accomplish this, she decides to get out of the tub with the jets blasting. During her first attempt to do this, she slips back into the tub and finds herself completely submerged under water. Finally she is able to sit up but her waist-length hair has become mangled and twisted. Looking like someone from a horror film, she manages to eventually drag her half limp body out of the tub. Not really wanting to wake anyone up to get instructions on how to work the tub, Lauren decides to do what she always does, try to take care of the problem herself. Playing with all the buttons, she finally manages to silence the tub, and exhausted, drags herself back into the huge bed to sleep. All the lights are off and she is beginning to doze off, when the tub suddenly turns itself back on. Returning to the bathroom to silence the tub, she is somehow able to turn it off again, or so she thinks. After climbing back into the bed again and trying to return to sleep, she hears the tub turn on again. She is tired, she wants to sleep, and this demonic bathtub continues to turn itself on about every fifteen to twenty minutes, just giving Lauren enough time to snuggle in and fall asleep before she is reawakened. Finally, at 1:30 A.M. in the morning, when all the rest of the house is asleep, Lauren makes the decision to fill the tub back up with water and let the tub do whatever it wants. That will work, won't it? Oh no, it can't be that easy!

As Lauren is refilling the tub, the jets turn on with the water not quite over the air holes yet. Yes, the water soaks the entire bathroom including Lauren. At this point, all Lauren can do is smile and wait for the tub to fill. She dries off, closes the bathroom door, and is serenaded to sleep by a Jacuzzi tub until 5:15 in the morning, time to get up and start the day.

Not just the bath tub incident, but the entire trip proves to be extraordinary. Bill and Susan Casner not only offer Lauren incredible hospitality, but a monthly sponsorship for three years to help her get to Beijing. Lauren is flabbergasted.

I think she explains it best herself, " I, who am still trying to learn to accept simple help from people, find generosity from people with no monetary value attached difficult to understand. Nevertheless, as hard as it is, I am learning to be able to accept the help of others. I only hope I am able to keep on sharing my experiences and help many along the way."

The challenge of the Jacuzzi tub, as funny as it seems now, is a metaphor for the little things an able-bodied person tries to do every day that become a huge hurdle for Lauren. Despite this, she does them, thriving, not shriveling, in the face of her daily trials.

Chapter 10

Problems are relative, simple as that. What might be a crisis for one person can be a small bump in the road for someone else. A splinter, a bad hair day or running out of ice cream could signal the complete ruin of an otherwise beautiful day for some. Slogging through Pagosa Springs' mud at the 2006 Savvy Conference with ooze sucking at cowboy boots and the annoyance of getting out the umbrella ever present, Lauren wheels around in her wheelchair with very little assistance and a smile on her face. She's dancing at the dance thrown by the Parellis on Saturday night and enjoying the Savvy Club experience without complaint. Watching her puts the weather and so many things in perspective. The clay-like mud suddenly doesn't seem so sticky. Living up to her philosophy that you take what life offers you and make the best of it, Lauren is enjoying the conference but is not prepared for the huge surprise Pat throws at her on Sunday during the final performance.

Since the 2005 Savvy Conference, Lauren, still living in Canada, has continued with her training and competing internationally. And as a true professional, she is always ready to take her skills to the next level. With ten minutes warning, Pat lets Lauren know that he wants to do a lesson in front of the whole crowd with both she and River, the beautiful white mare Lauren later was to think she was taking to the Paralympics. Pat often comments that prior and proper preparation prevent piss-poor performance. Lauren asks herself is she prepared for this. In spite of her lack of prior preparation, she is dressed and good to go complete with her radiant smile and a couple of helpers. Pat asks the audience if they are ready for something really special. Of course when they see Lauren wheeling into the arena on her own, the crowd goes crazy. They know they are truly in for something exceptional, just no idea what. Two helpers finish wheeling Lauren to the center of the arena and River is brought in as well. Pat gives Lauren a carrot stick, a long orange stick with heavy string on the end used to communicate better with the horse in the Parelli Natural Horsemanship Program, and River and Lauren begin to play. Lauren can't move in the deep sand, but she uses her carrot stick to send River out to circle her and play other games to help them become partners. Lovingly rubbing her face and body with her hands, Lauren conveys to River that she is her partner and will treat her with respect. After playing at liberty, without halter or lead line, Lauren feels the time is right to get on her and ride with Pat as her coach.

There is a fun little exchange between Pat and Lauren before she is assisted onto River. Pat wants a microphone on her during this experience, so he drops one down the front of her shirt.

Lauren says, "Cool", and Pat responds with, "Don't worry. I'm a professional."

Lauren quips back, "That's what I'm worried about!"

Lots of laughing from the audience as they begin to glimpse Lauren's quirky sense of humor. But there's more. As the helpers are assisting Lauren on River, she tells them to push her butt. She lets them, and the audience, know that this is a free grab.

She adds, "And I don't even get to enjoy it!"

Last minute tack adjustments are made and Pat asks her if she wants to start without her sticks. She says she will, and Pat asks her how many times she has ridden River. She says once and she has played with her three times before this lesson. Before they continue Pat asks Lauren if she wants to just go to the Paralympics or win the Paralympics.

Emphatically she responds, "Win!"

Pat continues and questions Lauren about dressage horses she has ridden in the past. He asks her to describe the problems she's had.

"Heavy," is her answer. She continues, "The horses have been heavy. They need a lot of leg and a lot of hand. My ride time on these horses has been limited to twenty minutes and then the horse falls apart. They need to be ridden regularly by my trainer or I can't keep them together." Pat wants to know what makes River and Magic different. Lauren is quick to respond, "They get better and better as the ride progresses."

Without her sticks, Lauren begins to move River out into the arena, Pat asking for a trot. She isn't sure he is talking to her, but he is. She blurts out, "Everybody trot." Again the crowd is laughing. This is going to be fun for the audience and Lauren. But the fun is just getting started. Pat offers techniques that Lauren can use to move her horse through the different gaits without legs. Focus, breathing, use of the reins all contribute to some amazing extended trots, half passes, the canter, transitions up and down, changes in direction, then a flying change. The crowd is on their feet exploding into applause.

Pat is ecstatic, Lauren is smiling from ear to ear, and he exclaims, "That smile's worth a million dollars to me folks."

Lauren, overwhelmed, responds with a simple, "Thanks Pat!"

Karen Rolf, a dressage expert and Parelli Professional who has been working with River, comes out in the arena to share in the joy and gives Lauren a hug. Lauren knows without a doubt that the Parelli program is helping her live her dream. Each and every day she is discovering the potential she has within her. And River will play a big part in this dream. Lauren remembers well the day she met this mare and realized she was full of expression, enthusiastic to please, yet extremely gentle. Pat and Linda think River might be just the horse for Lauren. They may be right!

LAUREN WITH RIVER AT LIBERTY

PAT PARELLI, LAUREN AND RIVER AT SAVVY CONFERENCE 2006

Chapter 11

After the Savvy Conference, September 2006, Lauren travels down to Florida to the Parellis' winter facility for a two week course sponsored by a Parelli student. At this time Pat and Linda ask her if she wants to have extended quality time with them in preparation for her pursuit of competing in Beijing, 2008. They would offer her a full sponsorship to do this. She would train with them in both Colorado and Florida for the next two years. After a two day interview in February, 2007, with Pat, Linda and Mark Weiler, the president of Parelli Natural Horsemanship, the mutual decision is made that yes, Lauren will do this. It is another huge leap of faith. She returns to Canada and in March of 2007 quits her job of five years at the Royal Bank of Canada, closes up her house, puts her stuff in storage, says good-by to friends, family, her support group and goes to train with Pat.

Making this transition in her life is huge for Lauren. She is not only going to Florida to continue her education as a top-level competitor in readiness for the biggest equestrian competition in the world, but she is hoping to find herself, claim her independence, find out what she believes in and who she wants to be. She needs this. Her coach in Canada, Sandra Verda, has been available to her 24/7, and so many other people and resources were easily accessible to help her as needed. Despite this, Lauren packs up her whole life, leaves this support system she has built over the seven years after her injury all in pursuit of independence, personal growth, and a discovery of just who is Lauren Barwick.

She is leaving the place her dad had lovingly helped her paint, remembering fondly Christmas 2005 and doing Christmas baking. While building a gingerbread house, she decided to paint her house. Her dad came over and noticed she had paint everywhere on every wall and she was overwhelmed.

Her dad asked her, "Why would you start something like this at this time of the year?"

Lauren's response was, "Why not?"

She loves her home. She has put up mirrors and has her favorite colors in the office and bedroom. Her dad's neighbor has even made her a beautiful dresser for her room. She is saying good-bye to this place of her own.

The hardest good-bye of all, though, is her good-bye to Shelby, her dog. Shelby became part of Lauren's life in 2001. She had been a police dog in training and was at the top of her class. Before going to Alberta for her final stage of training, she was tested and found to have Lupus. Lauren's mother heard that she was going to be put down and thought she would be a great canine companion and assistant for Lauren. To have her, Lauren had to agree to have her spayed. As a result of the operation, Shelby became very sick. Skin and bones, Lauren was only able to get her to drink milk shakes and had to give her the medication she needed through a straw. One day when Lauren went out to her van, Shelby lay down on the lift and wouldn't move. She didn't have the strength to jump up in the van and didn't want Lauren to leave her. That was the day the bond really developed between this smart dog and loving human.

Shelby did get well, and, with the help of a dog trainer for the disabled, she was able to go to work with Lauren at the bank. The customers loved her. She would carry their bank books to Lauren and back. People would bring her Frisbees and treats every day. She was a great topic of conversation in an environment where people might not have been comfortable talking to Lauren because of her disability. Shelby put them at ease. Although she was Lauren's best friend, she had to stay in Canada as well. Lauren's mom took Shelby in, and Shelby later found a home where she could be a companion to a woman who had a husband with Parkinson's disease. Shelby would get to go to the hospital and make many people smile, but the parting for Lauren was tearful. Lauren is leaving all that she had known for the unknown and a horse named River. She is losing her best friend in a painful exchange for a once in a lifetime shot at greatness.

Returning to the Parelli ranch in Ocala, moving in to an apartment in Pat's barn, Lauren spends the next six months building a relationship with River in the hope she will carry her all the way to the Summer Paralympics. Lauren realizes that River is extremely sensitive, learning quickly to respond to all of Lauren's aids. With a slight click under Lauren's breath, River extends her movement just enough. In tune with her slightest request, Lauren feels like she is wearing the perfect glove. What could possibly happen to mar this perfection?

During her training time with River, Pat and Lauren become concerned about the horse's over all soundness. When she arrives home from an amazing performance in Australia with Pat, she just doesn't seem consistently one hundred per cent. This makes both Lauren and Pat uneasy; if she makes it to the Paralympics there will be a vet check making sure all horses competing are doing so completely sound. One of River's hocks is fusing and the campaign for the Paralympics will be stressful. During 2007, Lauren and River compete well, with a first in the National Show in Langley, B.C. and a second in the BC Provincial Games, in Maple Ridge, BC. Nevertheless, the decision has to be made whether River is going or not. Lauren qualifies for the Canadian Team, but she has to qualify a horse as well.

She has also been riding Dior in Canada to qualify for the team. In fact, she won a first place medal on him in the BC Games. As she is struggling with a hard choice about River, she learns that Dior has a recurring infection in his leg that will require that he be put down. This is a very emotional loss for Lauren. As she reflects, "I learned a lot from him. He developed me into a strong rider. I was very fortunate that his owner, Andrea Taylor, allowed him to teach me so much. My last time seeing him all I could do was thank him. He had been my dancing partner for four years. We had achieved many of my dreams and goals together."

Compounding the loss Lauren feels for Dior is making the final decision regarding River. With tears in her eyes during a quiet moment with this magnificent horse she tells her, "Sorry, Sweetie, you don't get to go to the party of a lifetime."

And this takes us back to where we started this story of an incredible young woman, her quest for the Paralympic Gold and finding the perfect horse to take her there.

Chapter 12

I can tell you what finding the perfect horse is not. It is not shopping for the perfect car. There are certain constants and tangibles in car buying. Not so with horses. Athleticism, conformation, overall health might compare to kicking the tires, but then you have sensitivity to the rider, innate intelligence, and that whole relationship thing. The stress of competing can strain the rapport between horse and rider, sometimes to the breaking point. Lauren knows how important the intangible connections between horse and rider can be. She has a tool belt full of extraordinary tools she has acquired from the Parellis to help her to become a champion. Can she find a horse that will give her the opportunity to use these tools? Where can she find a horse that can help her finish the journey she started so long ago?

She thinks about using Peanut, her horse she competed on in jumping before the accident, the horse she started Parelli Natural Horsemanship with. But Peanut isn't really a valid back up. She has lots of emotional issues from being leased out during Lauren's hospital stay. By December of 2007, Lauren has no choice and no horse. She has to continue competing to keep her Canadian ranking, so she pulls Peanut out of a field and starts getting her ready but with reservations. Peanut is a jumping mare, and this new course of events, Lauren feels, will not be mentally fair to her. Lauren loves Peanut. Her emotional rock is how she refers to her. This is a true dilemma resulting in the decision not to use Peanut in the end.

Certainly the search will continue for the perfect horse to go on to Beijing. Lauren's criteria in addition to appearance and ability, is that the horse has a natural go button, knows its responsibility to maintain gait, and has a light and sensitive mouth. In addition the horse must tolerate Lauren's dressage sticks. The large, lofty trot of a Warmblood is preferable.

To assist in this incredibly difficult search, Linda Parelli sends out a mass e mail to all the Parelli associate trainers and instructors with their program requesting leads on possible horses. Pat also introduces Lauren to David O'Conner, an American Oylmpian. David offers to let Lauren try his lovely grey horse Walk on the Moon (Danny). She is honored. After a few rides they decide to give him a test run at an upcoming competition. Lauren travels over to the O'Conners four to five days a week until the middle of January, 2008. It is not an easy transition for a horse to go from being ridden with legs for most of his life to having zero guidance or communication coming from the human's lower half, but Danny proves to be a trooper. He is very obedient but not extremely motivated to go forward. The first show goes well, the judges think Lauren and Danny make a smashing couple, but mention that the horse needs more forward energy. Lauren feels that improving the forward movement is achievable, but since it isn't natural for the horse, it makes riding him was more difficult than it needs to be. She also feels that having to push him so forward might break their relationship. Lauren knows that she and Danny will not work out.

Lauren rides Peanut at this show as well and does remarkably well. She even achieves a qualifying score for Beijing. However in her first class Peanut's emotions get the better of her. She does some lovely Piaffe, which would have been totally acceptable except that they are supposed to be walking. Peanut will continue as the back-up for now, but the hunt for the perfect horse continues.

Thanks to the wonders of the internet, Lauren, unbeknownst to Pat and Linda, finds Maile, a fourteen year old Dutch Warmblood, located in the Orlando area. She arranges a first ride for January 2008. She lets the owners know she has some leg weaknesses, just doesn't happen to mention that she is paralyzed from the waist down. Lauren is worried that the owners might not even give her a chance if they know that. She sent them lots of photos of her riding and some articles about herself prior to her visit. When she arrives and it is obvious she is paralyzed, the owners want to see her ride with a lunge line first.

After the first ride Lauren exclaims, "I can win a medal on this horse!"

Not only is Maile a flashy mare, but she has courage, heart and willingness, traits that this horse will prove she has over and over again in the following year leading up to the Paralympics in September. Maile means Hawaiian flower, and this Maile is a beauty with a sweet disposition to match. Lauren has a strong feeling that this might be the horse she is searching for. Lauren rides Maile two more times, and is surprised at how much she is capable of doing with this mare in such a short time and how well she adapts to "no legs". Wheels were turning in Lauren's head, as she imagines how much she can accomplish when Maile is in "Pat's world of Natural Horsemanship". She takes a video of her, sends it to the Parellis and arranges a vet check. If Maile passes, Pat will lease her with the option to buy at any time. Questions remain. Will this beautiful bay mare with the sweetest of dispositions be able to carry Lauren all the way to her dream? Will Maile understand not just Lauren's cues but her hopes and fears along this challenging journey? Will they be able to partner up and compete in harmony? And would she be sound? Through Pat's excellent negotiating skills, Maile is leased by the Parellis with the option to buy conditional upon passing the vet check and the trot up exam at the Paralympics. The deal is made and Lauren begins her partnership with Maile, or The Bird, as she's called in the barn. She is now Lauren's to play with and ride. She has found a horse.

But as with many seemingly perfect endings, there is a problem with the vet check at Pat's. Maile is found to have a mild stringhalt, a neurological disorder that causes an exaggerated step with one of the back legs. It is an irregularity at the trot that some vets might consider lameness, but in Maile's case, it goes away as soon as she is ridden. The trot up exam at the Paralympics, though, is done from the ground and therefore this is of some concern preparing for Hong Kong, the now determined site for the equestrian events during the Olympic and Paralympic Games. Over the next few months, Lauren takes the horse to two FEI (Federation Equestrian International) vets for trot up exams just like she would have in Hong Kong. She passes both of them and Lauren receives letters stating this is the case. She starts to feel a little more confident. And thank goodness because she started bonding with Maile right away. She is smart and affectionate. She adapts to Lauren's disability remarkably quickly especially for a horse that has been ridden with legs her whole life.

Things were not perfect near the beginning, but Lauren and Maile progress. Lauren remembers trying to halter Maile from her scooter. Their first day together at the ranch, it was a huge challenge for Maile to get her head down so Lauren could get a halter on. It took twenty minutes. You can only imagine how hard it was to bridle her. A few months later, Lauren was bridling her on her own and quickly. Meeting Maile personally in August of 2008, I noticed Lauren could not get her out of her lap. They have a very special horse-human bond nurtured by natural horsemanship that foreshadows upcoming success. Maile is described by Lauren as a busy body, wanting to know what all the other horses are doing. But this motherly trait transfers to Lauren. Lauren really believes that Maile's devotion to her is an innate understanding of her disability. With Maile frequently nuzzling and hovering over her, Lauren believes they are developing a special relationship, and she knows if this happens, she and Maile can make it all the way to Hong Kong 2008.

Maile also came to the Parelli ranch unconfident. She was afraid of the miniature horses, Barnum and Bailey, she was afraid of cows, and she was worried about warm up arenas if other horses were there and passing her. Some of these problems were fixed from the ground; some were worked out with time spent. People at the ranch would comment that they knew the cows were nearby or going by because they could hear Maile snorting like a whale.

Lauren says that Maile would have a disgusting look on her face when she was asked to move cows as if to say, "I'm a dressage horse. I don't do this."

But she didn't get away with this on Pat's ranch. The horses there work cows. Pat rode Maile in his western saddle with the cows at his ranch and this would pay off in Hong Kong where many new exciting things would be waiting, much scarier than cows. Maile and Lauren developed confidence over the next few months in preparation for the dream of a lifetime.

Chapter 13

Lauren had qualified for the 2008 Paralympics but Maile had not. With so little time, five months, Lauren and Maile have to accomplish a miracle. At the Ocala Winter Dressage Show, January 19th and 20th, just a couple of weeks after Maile's arrival at the ranch the first week of January, these new partners are off to make this miracle happen.

Lauren has natural ability and a strong focus. She has enhanced those skills with Pat Parelli's Natural Horsemanship Program. She has found a fantastic horse, she has qualified for the Canadian Para-Equestrian Team, but Maile must qualify for them both to make the team. This is where the great master, Walter Zettl, steps up to assist. He has produced so many Olympic medal winners and has spent so much time working with the Parellis that he seems to be an ideal fit. His comments about Lauren are complimentary.

He says, "I have much respect for this young lady because she has no feeling in her legs, but has a very good seat and is a very good rider. She's an amazing young lady. She also has a great mind and ability to focus and she tries to do everything that one says."

He has such immense admiration for her riding skills that he often asks her for the posting trot, forgetting that she can't.

She says, "I love it when he does that!"

They begin to work together with Mr. Zettl commenting on the great foundation she has had with the natural horsemanship approach she has incorporated into her dressage style. Patience and not rushing the horse are a huge part of his secret to success and Lauren finds this comforting. He gives Lauren three lessons. With such an accomplished and distinguished dressage master to help her, Lauren works on her attitude and confidence. Impressing him, he calls her an amazing young lady; they join forces to qualify Maile, using the Ocala Winter Dressage Show at the Florida Horse Park as a starting point. The stress is overwhelming, and she is afraid she will communicate this to her smart, sensitive mare.

She asks, "What's four years of dedication, sacrifice and hard work, all tested in a six minute performance? No pressure!"

Helping to relieve this pressure is the incredible mutual admiration Walter Zettl and Lauren have for each other and the Parelli Natural Horsemanship program. Zettl believes that the natural horsemanship approach has given Lauren the effective tools that will easily carry her into the upcoming Paralympics. Lauren is equally impressed with him.

"He's fabulous," she says of the master. "He has a wonderful approach. Instead of forcing your horse to do it, it just happens naturally and the horse offers you so much more. With Walter's approach, the horses look happy because they are happy."

At this moment, Lauren needs Maile to be happy. She has only ridden her six times before the Ocala Show. Getting used to no legs, just sticks, was a huge adjustment for a horse that had been ridden her whole life with legs. Maile does make the adjustment achieving two of the three qualifying scores needed affirming to Lauren that this mare is a true champion at heart and can be her Paralympic partner. Ocala is a huge success and the impetus to continue the journey to Hong Kong.

Describing this test ride, Lauren has said, "The mare did great! Her scores aren't medal level yet, but this gives us a place to build from. There are a lot of things I'd like to work on, but that's just her getting used to me. She's really a very good mare, very understanding and very willing and very forgiving. That's what I like about her."

Lauren's support system at this critical time in her life was diverse ranging from great teachers to great friends, and one very important member of this team was her roommate, Jenna Cody. Jenna helped Lauren at her competitions and rode her horses around the show grounds for her periodically. Lauren and Jenna chuckle when they think about Jenna's background in barrel racing and having never ridden in English riding pants before. Jenna learned very quickly that full leather breeches should not be worn with a thong, and she soon invested in full bottom underwear. Jenna was also a much needed sounding board for Lauren when she would verbally rage or when she was just plain tired of wondering if things would work out.

Once when Lauren was slowly slipping to the floor transferring from her shower chair to her manual chair, Jenna demonstrated true friendship. Lauren called to her for help. Jenna came running into the bathroom, picked her up and slung her back in her chair. Lauren remembers giving her a horrified look because she had anticipated that Jenna would grab her under her arms, but, in the moment, she scooped her up by grabbing her bare bottom. They continue to laugh about this to this day.

One tragic crack in their friendship did occur when a friend of Lauren's life was lost in a fatal accident that involved Jenna. Or was it a murder? An abundance of wildlife lives in Florida, including cockroaches. A very special cockroach, named Bob by Lauren, would visit with Lauren while she was in the toilet for an hour in the morning. Because she was sitting for such a long period Bob wasn't just a friend but a distraction. Jenna not only did not understand their friendship, but she wanted Bob exterminated. Late one dark night, Jenna got up to use the washroom and came across Bob. The details are not clear, but Lauren found her beloved friend squished dead on the floor the next day. To emphasize the criminal intent of this act, Lauren sketched out a crime scene of his body with chalk, writing "Hit and Run" by his pathetic, lifeless body. Poor Bob! Jenna and Lauren's friendship survived this traumatic event and is so dear that Lauren will become Jenna's bridesmaid at her wedding.

Other elements during this time also bring a smile to Lauren's lips. She humorously describes how she was able to have undemanding time with not only Maile but all her horses. She credits her power chair for this. Apparently it does not do well in the deep sand in Florida. She has spent a lot of time hanging out with horses, stuck, waiting for someone to save her. She has considered having a horse pull her out, however with the chair being barely four hundred pounds the probability of the horse pulling her body out of the chair was more likely to happen than getting the chair out of the sand. Having a fifteen hundred pound animal tied to her power chair is not a comforting notion.

Along with the difficulties with the chair, Lauren realized she needed a new saddle. She and Linda Parelli worked for eight months on developing a new dressage saddle during this period of preparing for the Paralympics. Lauren says she sat in a lot of different saddles, had Velcro rolls stuck to all different parts of her lower body, had different straps everywhere, had shims removed and added, rode different horses, worked on finding her balance point, twisted her body right, left, back and forward, used white tape, duct tape and many giggles were involved. At this point in time, she had not yet seen the final product and was extremely excited to see the result of all their efforts.

At the end of January, Lauren and Maile were off to what they hoped would be the last leg of their qualification journey, Wellington in West Palm Beach. Joining them would be Mollie Robbins, the head of horse health with the Parelli organization, to assist Lauren. Wellington would give Lauren and Maile an awesome opportunity to prepare for the type of weather Hong Kong could throw at them. Describing the weather as rainy would be an understatement. The water actually came up to her wheel chair cushion. Lauren relates that knowing her cushion could also be used as a floatation device gave her some peace of mind. The weather even affected Maile who with her lovely, expressive movement, thought she might be too much of a lady to be dancing in a foot of water. Lauren is sure she thought she was going to wreck her "manicure", not to mention dirtying her four stunning white legs. Despite the weather, Lauren had one main focus and that was to achieve one more championship score so that Maile would be officially qualified and the show was a total success. She competed in an FEI Open Class, which combined many different levels of riders from Grand Prix to FEI Pony; there were twenty-one in the class. The horses were phenomenal with many good riders. She remembers thinking that she needed to just think about her goal, achieving a qualifying score, but she was shocked and pleased to find out she had won the class! She was happy but most of all relieved that she had done what she had set out to do, and now she and Maile could continue working on making their foundation solid.

She says, "I wanted to develop Maile from a nice Lexus to a fine Ferrari, a smooth ride where we truly looked like a unified pair moving as one."

Lauren mentions, describing this period in their training, that one of the hardest things for her to do was trust in the process, allow the natural stages of developing a horse to happen and try not to skip stages. Hard to do when deadlines loom in the near future. But she did trust, and all of a sudden Maile began to offer more advanced movements, things that Lauren knew she had the potential to do and they were happening naturally. June 4, 2008, would be the final deadline for submitting qualifying scores. By the end of that June, Canada would select the four riders who would be on the Para-Equestrian Team representing their country in Hong Kong. Lauren continued to compete to develop herself and her horse so that they would peak when it really counted.

Other challenges, while in Florida, would also occur to develop Lauren's stamina and test Lauren's ambition to achieve great things. Actually they would be something a lot more down to earth than dressage movements, like overcoming her fear of tornado warnings that would crop up on the television screen. Florida is famous for its tornados and Lauren and her roommates had a deal. If a tornado touched down, her roommates would duct tape her to her wheelchair and hand her riding helmet to her. On one occasion, this wasn't possible and Lauren had to recover from being swallowed by a storm. She was rapidly wheeling through the horizontal rain and hit a foot of sand that didn't belong where it was on the driveway. Proceeding to flip out of her chair, she found herself on a rather gritty water slide down the driveway. She did get back in her floating wheel chair eventually, and struggled her way to her van. She discovered her electric door and ramp remote were no longer functioning and began to think that perhaps being submerged in water tends to prevent electrical things from working. She dragged herself in through the passenger door, heaved her chair in behind her and finished this endeavor with a good cursing session followed by hysterical laughter.

She commented, "What fun! I always look forward to my daily test of do I really have the desire?"

Ocala Spring Dressage at the Florida Horse Park in Ocala, Florida, was the last big show Lauren competed in before she would be returning to Canada for quarantine and to train with the Canadian Team. With a dramatic finish as only Lauren can conjure up, she was competing in tornado warning weather. Maile's tail was flying horizontally, and she had to hold on to her saddle to keep from falling off. She says when she headed in certain directions she couldn't breathe. This show was a remarkable turning point for her personal mare, Peanut. They had an excellent first level test, placing third out of ten, and Peanut actually walked.

Lauren remarked, "As much as I am impressed with her ability to piaffe, a walk is thrilling. I will admit that it could have been the G-force winds pushing against us, but all I could think about was that she did it and at the end of the test I was so happy, content and proud of her. I left the ring thinking I could stop riding all together, leaving with this exhilarating feeling."

The Ocala Spring Dressage and that "feeling" helped Lauren to realize something about her emotional and mental fitness when she competes.

Thoughtfully she explains, "When I ride Peanut there is no pressure. When we make a technical mistake I laugh about it. I'm smiling throughout the test, and at the end of it I can feel good about what we accomplished. It is quite the opposite when I ride Maile. I feel as if there is an immense amount of pressure for everything to be perfect. I'm so focused that I start to become rigid, stiff and direct lined. I beat myself up in the test when I make a mistake, making our next movements fall apart. I'm going into each test knowing this ride could be the difference between whether I am on the team or not."

So Lauren is off to Canada again. Her goal for the next three months will be to find love, fun and satisfaction in herself and her horse. She will need to go into the ring with the confidence that they are ready, prepared and dancing for a score of ten while smiling through the whole test. Lauren knows that Maile can feel her attitude and her confidence. She is a smart, sensitive mare and will need Lauren to be a great leader and believe in her so that she can do her job.

Lauren often reflects on a quote that motivates her by Ralph Marston, "Overcoming the unexpected and discovering the unknown is what ignites our spirit. It is what life is all about… It's what you do today that will matter tomorrow…"

In Canada, the weight of the unexpected and unknown as well as some personal challenges will set the stage for Lauren and Maile's success or failure in Hong Kong.

JENNA ON MAILE AND LAUREN ON PEANUT

Chapter 14

Returning to Canada hoping to become a member of the Canadian Para-Equestrian Team for 2008 with a new horse, a new saddle, and new techniques, Lauren is filled with renewed hope and resolve. She had gone to the USA on the Parelli Scholarship to find herself. Can she sustain the feeling of independence and purpose she had found now that she is returning to Canada? If asked to be a part of Team Canada she will be following the program of the team manager and team coaches. Can she do this and keep her core values intact? Huge challenges and compromises loom in her future at this point. Her toughness and stamina will be tested greatly.

To secure her spot on the Canadian Team, Lauren will need to receive high scores at the Canadian Nationals which she begins preparing for on her return. She is successful, scoring 74.86, 75 and 76.9, and on June 4, 2008, Lauren is proud to announce that she has secured a spot on the team. Both she and Maile have qualified for this great honor and now they are a team that is part of a team that will go down in Canadian history. Each team member is riding their own horse for the first time. The time for borrowed horses is over.

Now this dream of Lauren's is beginning to take shape and become a reality. She is going to the Paralympics in Hong Kong, and she finds herself experiencing many feelings, realizing that the emotional side of a competitive journey like this is exhausting. Her emotional fitness is being put to the test.

Lauren lists just some of the emotions that are pulsing through her at this point in her odyssey. She starts with: "Excitement, when I discover true unity and partnership resulting in an amazing ride; fear of letting everyone down who believes in me; doubt in myself and my horse; confidence when I get that reaffirmation from my mentors and the judges; nausea every time I get an e mail with the riders' new rankings; panic with every new deadline; dread if my horse ever takes a sore step and love when my mare looks up at me from the pasture; amazement when I realize what she allows me to do with her; sadness when I ask myself if I am doing what is best for my horse or am I just thinking about my final goal; guilt when asking myself if I am good enough; empowerment when I realize where I was and what my potential is. But most of all I feel fortunate, knowing I have a team of people doing their best to help me succeed. I wake up in the middle of the night my mind alive with the question, what if?"

Part of the "what if" is the succession of adverse daily obstacles that Lauren seems to face and overcome and people seem to question. Lauren's answer to them is, honestly, because she is out there doing things most people in wheelchairs don't do. Lauren's father says she does more than a walking person which is a lot in one day. She is not accident prone; she is trying to be productive in a difficult situation. She describes her learning process, for example learning to saddle a horse from her wheel chair, as comprising several steps. For her to figure out how to do something she needs to try different things. There may be a first, second or possibly a third attempt, all of which may not be successful and leave her in a compromised position or in the dirt. For her doing, not watching, is the key to learning. She discovers what she can do, what is possible and what she can achieve. Learning from your mistakes is part of this process as well, and Lauren can tell you from experience there are a lot of wrong ways to do something. Lauren even knows all the wrong ways to saddle her horse from her wheelchair. Yes, she can saddle a horse up to sixteen three hands, but before success it was a disaster for both her and her saddle. She has confidence now that she can do it and may drop it on her face from time to time, or fall from her chair during the process, or end up with the horse standing on her. But that is not the point, she believes. It's that she's doing something, something thought not to be possible.

Mark Weiler, President of Parelli Natural Horsemanship, calls this quality in Lauren "grit". Mark watched Lauren, one day when they were all down at the Parelli Ranch in Florida, fall over a bump going down a road from her lodging to the stable area. She came out of her wheelchair and fell. Realizing she was bloody and hurt, people that witnessed this event including Mark came running down the road to help her.

She said, "Stop right there!"

Mark replied, "You don't have to do this."

Lauren's response was, "Yes I do!"

Yes, she does. She has to prove to herself and the world that she can do anything she sets her mind to including winning a gold medal in the Paralympics in Hong Kong. This is the culmination of an arduous journey she has taken to turn a possible life-long tragedy into a triumph. Lauren and Maile are on the Canadian Para-Equestrian Team. They are on their way to Hong Kong.

Backtracking just a little, Lauren's return trip to Canada with four horses and two friends is something not to be forgotten. What should have been a four day trip turned into five because of a bright idea of Lauren's. She really didn't want Mike Decristoforo, the barn manager, and Lyndsey Fitch, a Parelli intern who would be Lauren's groom and support, to miss the "real Rockies". She thought they should take a detour through Alberta, Canada. She realized after about two hours of being wowed by their size and beauty that she had forgotten what the Rockies were like. This turned into a fourteen hour marathon with everyone, including the horses, fed up and wondering when the "real Rockies" were going to end.

Lauren was traveling with four of her horses, the youngest being Ben, a one year old. As Lauren tells it, he started out the trip like an excited youngster looking at everything and ended up lying down. She says he gave up saying, "Are we there yet?" and spent the next week sleeping. Lauren describes Ben as cheeky, in your face, goofy, adorable and very large. She imagines him as an adolescent boy who spends his days at the skate board park using the word, "dude". Peanut, Hungarian Cayenne, Lauren's fourteen year old Hungarian mare is sensitive to the max. She does not like to be bothered and wonders why Lauren is doing this to her. She did not want Ben touching her, and had had enough after day one. Maile and West Point were a whole other story. Maile, who had been a mother mare before, decided that West Point could be her boyfriend. West Point, a big handsome German Hanovarian gelding, could have cared less about Maile except that he was fed up that he was covered in slobber. Maile traveled the best of the four because she had her boy-toy, West Point, to amuse her. He, on the other hand, thought he deserved special treatment. Where was the air-conditioning, why aren't there air shocks, where is the permanent water? He didn't want to eat, he didn't want to drink, and he couldn't be tied this way or that way. Lauren asked the age-old question, why is it the most expensive horses cause the most grief?

Lauren makes it back to her most recent home town of Langley about a week before the Nationals. She and her horses need the opportunity to work with both the national coach, Andrea Taylor, and her personal coach, Sandra Verda. Additionally this is her chance to see how she fares against her possible fellow team mates and to improve her overall ranking for the actual selection. She enters three horses in the show, Maile, Peanut, and West Point, her new purchase she has never competed on. Looking back on this day, Lauren asks herself what she was thinking. Perhaps her super woman complex had kicked in trying to convince her that she would have a never-ending abundance of energy that would allow her to compete for three days in five classes each day. She scratches West Point and focuses on Maile and Peanut. This is probably a very good decision because things are not as she had hoped at this point.

In the warm up on Maile, the mare is throwing her head in the air and Lauren is feeling, as she puts it, discombobulated. Lauren is confused, the mare is tense and they have to go in the ring. As she is heading up the center line, she remembers clearly thinking how absolutely angry she was and continued to be throughout the entire test. She thinks she looked horrible, she doesn't need this kind of stress in her life and she is quitting. Of course, she made mistakes in her accuracy since the competition ring was the last place her mind was. Outside of the ring she realizes that she had competed at eight shows already that year and not once had she gone in the ring frustrated or angry. Why is this happening today of all days?

As Lauren and Peanut enter the ring after a terrible warm up, Lauren knows she can't continue. After thirty seconds,

Lauren turns Peanut towards the judge, halts, bows her head and dismisses herself. Embarrassment doesn't even begin to describe how she feels as the home town girl no one has seen for a year, and she feels she has not represented the Parelli Program well. To Lauren's surprise, Lindsey is on the sidelines applauding her. She tells Lauren how proud she is of her for doing what is best for her horse. Again, Lauren asks herself what happened.

Lauren remembers the lack of motivation that had turned her back to Parelli Natural Horsemanship. She remembers why she went to the Parelli Program on a scholarship. She remembers the fantastic results she has had on Maile so far this year and with other Parelli horses she has ridden and competed on. What changed? Two worlds have collided at this point. The traditional dressage methods Lauren was originally trained in and the different ideas that she has brought home with her. She knows how much she learned from her personal coach who took her all the way to Athens, and she knows how much confidence and knowledge she exudes now with different techniques from Parelli Natural Horsemanship. How can she bring the two together to get to Hong Kong? She does not want to force her horses, she wants to take the time it takes and not rush the process and she wants both she and her horse to feel relaxed in an enjoyable partnership. This is a conundrum that would not be solved easily or painlessly for Lauren.

The afternoon after these disastrous performances, Lauren has said she hid like an injured animal, licking her wounds. She finally got up the nerve to go get her test scores from her ride on Maile. She is shocked when she sees her score of seventy-six per cent, one judge giving her a seventy-eight. These are huge scores, the highest of the three riders being trained by Lauren's coach. She does not quit, but she is ashamed of her riding and feels she did not preserve her horse's dignity. Bottom line, she feels she does not deserve the kindness and loyalty that Maile had shown her. Nevertheless, it is this sensibility and innate fairness to the horse that ultimately has led to Lauren's success.

Isn't there a saying somewhere about "the best laid plans..."? Well, why should Lauren's plans be any different? Plan A was to finish her competitions and return to a wonderful summer in Colorado to continue training with Pat Parelli and Walter Zettl. She felt this plan was crucial for her emotional sanity. Plan B came about in one word, quarantine! For sixty days, starting June 18, she and Maile would be in pre-quarantine with the other four horses named to the Canadian team. Maile and Lauren entered "jail" without the benefit of visitors. Lauren would have to give up living in her glorious, dusty cabin without plumbing, dodging lightning bolts with her power chair, bats, chipmunks in her van, gifts from mice on her pillow and bears casually crossing her path. This was the world she knew and had looked forward to. She was now about to enter a world that will take her half way around the globe to somewhere she can only imagine at this point.

Chapter 15

Being selected as a participant in the Paralympic Games might appear to some to be the pinnacle of glamour and glory. For Lauren and Maile they felt as if they had plummeted into an abyss where all personal freedoms were eliminated because of the billion dollar horse racing industry in Hong Kong, not necessarily for the protection of the team's horses. There was great fear of infectious diseases coming into China. All the specifics of this ordeal are too various to mention, but some examples will suffice to give an overall picture. Horses must not be within twelve feet of other horses at any time, human hands must be sanitized whenever entering the barn and no equipment can have been used on other horses, even the cleaning equipment had to be sanitized. People who handle the horses must be limited to the owner, coaches, the barn staff and vets. No trail riding is allowed and training is limited to certain pre-arranged times for a two hour period six days a week. The team is not allowed to compete because it puts the horses at risk. The vet checks the horses' vitals twice a month. If you can name it, as Lauren puts it, the horses are vaccinated against it. If they leave the premises, a federal vet would be required to sign them out and sign them back in.

The facility was not much easier to deal with than the conditions. Since there were limited places that could accommodate the team, they were given a little barn in a larger equestrian facility. The only turn-out was a one-quarter acre field and a twenty by twenty sand paddock along with a twenty by fifteen matted, covered enclosed stall looking out at the sand paddock. There were three horses in this quarantine area so they switched throughout the day between the three places. In addition to the already existing challenges, other riders at the center used this arena during the team's ride time and seemed to not like having riders with disabilities in the barn with them.

The first two weeks of quarantine were very difficult for the horses, but they did eventually settle in to a routine. Lauren, however, did not. Complicating her situation further, Lauren took a fall from her chair causing a bump on her seat bone that would keep her from riding for two and a half weeks. It did heal and Lauren resumed training unbothered by it, but it was definitely a set-back. Andrea and Sandra rode Maile during her recuperation while Lauren worried this could end up becoming something much worse.

One little spark of freedom during quarantine came in July with a mini day pass to the Amherst Dressage Show. This involved a large disinfected trailer and an indoor arena that was isolated for just the five riders on the team. They arrived at the competition grounds, tacked up, warmed up in the indoor arena, and were escorted to the competition ring, rode their test, then straight back to the indoor ring to cool down, un-tack, load up and return home to their jail. During all of this a national vet was observing to ensure none of the horses were compromised by contact with other humans or horses.

Saying that she has never done a horse show so quickly, Lauren felt like she was in a movie at fast forward. The good news was that she and Maile were able to compete in their brand new musical freestyle, choreographed by Karen Robinson of Applause Dressage. It went well; timing was excellent. They scored 71.99 per cent, the over-all freestyle high point of the show. Lauren likes powerful music and Karen put together a combination of Asian and New Age music that was perfect for the Hong Kong Paralympics.

Despite its strict boundaries, returning to quarantine left Lauren feeling lost. Army-like, it seemed as if there was no individuality, only tight timelines, horses were being marched from one stall or paddock to another. There was nowhere to play with horses or cross train. Everything was micro-managed and everything was out of her control. Lauren was spiraling toward a meltdown at this critical juncture in her life.

Lauren describes people saying to her, "Wow, you must be so excited. What an amazing journey! I'd give anything to be able to compete at that level."

In reality, she shares that this last leg of her "Riding for the Gold" journey has been extremely complex, emotional, and has pushed her to her breaking point.

In her words, "My heart has ached over the past four years more than I ever want to feel again. I wanted to achieve to the best of my ability more than anything ever. I knew I was capable of achieving gold but that involved all my little ducks being lined up in a perfect row. Looking back, I think I have always had a rogue duck in my line up. I'm thinking that little rogue duck decided to be a team player for this trip. Being that prepared, being able to be my absolute best for the six minutes I am in a ring in front of five judges requires a type of focus that does not come easily. At the end of each session, I found myself exhausted and very upset. All I wanted to do was sleep for the rest of the day. In eight years of training for the Paralympics, I had never had a problem with my focus, and now I was finding it very hard."

Lauren began to feel she needed to speak to someone about her mental and emotional "sport related problems". In other words, as she explains it, the technical term for losing her mind. Someone at the Fraser Valley Pacific Sport Center recommended a sports psychologist, Donna, and the dam that had been holding back so much in Lauren opened wide. The tears began to flow. Experienced in this field, Donna gave Lauren a clear description of what was going on and gave her some practical suggestions she could implement immediately, critical with a deadline for the competition of her lifetime looming. She had a mild identity crisis and mild depression. She was caught between two worlds, her old and the more traditional, and the new that she had found so much success with. Being a people pleaser and disabled puts Lauren in a compromised position, so they discussed who she was in that grey area. In contrast, her style is more "ride by the seat of her pants". So by adding more organization and a clear plan to her riding style she would become more balanced and not lose herself in the process. She learned to let people know she appreciated their opinions or ideas, but that she needed to do what she felt was best for her. And at the end of the day, **she** was the part of the equation that cannot be removed. That is a very strong card, and she realized, often forgotten.

At one month before leaving for the games, she is making some life changes; embracing her style, using imagery, realizing that her sport can relax her, and changing sleep patterns by not oversleeping when something horrible is going on. And something horrible was going on in addition to the hardships of quarantine. Lauren's wonderful Thoroughbred mare she had grown up riding had extreme complications giving birth. Princess herniated her whole right side. The vet gave her two days to live, and she had a two week early colt on the ground. Every two hours he had to be fed, antibiotics given to him and the mare, the mare's horse girdle tightened, the mare milked and temperatures taken for both horses. Lauren's friend, Shannon, took shifts with her. Lauren did the night and Shannon did the day while she slept and trained.

For the duration of her quarantine, Lauren continued providing care for Princess and her foal. The little colt has earned the name Platinum based on Lauren's Visa bill. The mare needed massive doses of pain killers and her baby needed buckets of milk and first-aid for an infected belly button and a raw bottom caused by diarrhea. Later having gone to the National Lacrosse Finals with her kids, Shannon could not relieve Lauren, and in addition, Lauren cared for Shannon's wandering dog, Brutus in her absence. And Lauren's power chair dies officially. She is left with her little granny scooter named Red. It worked, but not as well, until her power chair was repaired and returned. None of this stops Lauren, but this stress certainly chips away at her focus.

One of the training sessions found Lauren at the barn with very limited sleep saddling Maile. She came to the other side of the horse to adjust the saddle and instead pulled it down on top of her. The metal stirrup iron came down and landed on her face splitting her lip open wide. There were frothy, bloody bubbles everywhere and the saddle was under the horse. Lauren lost it and began screaming profanities along with, "I quit! I've had enough!" Cleaning herself up in the restroom thankfully gave her a chance to cool down. She returned to find poor Maile still standing in the barn with a saddle on the ground wondering if Lauren was ever coming back. Lauren did come back, as she always does no matter the level of difficulties she's facing, and had a wonderful ride on Maile, perhaps one of her best. She was so tired and emotionally burned out that she stopped fighting with the demons in her head. She became a passenger on Maile and let her fill in all the holes.

With great emotion Lauren shares, "Maile is an absolutely wonderful mare, and I am very grateful she has accompanied me on this journey. At this point she hadn't really revealed herself. Little did I know the strength she would soon share with me."

Princess is eventually put down, the foal survives but with some permanent lameness, and Lauren goes on to Hong Kong with a combination of optimism and a terrible weight on her shoulders.

Chapter 16

The last leg of the journey before Hong Kong has arrived, August 18, 2008. All five horses on the team are traveling to a small town outside of Santa Barbara, Solvang, California, to be in an even stricter quarantine at Monty Roberts' ranch. This will become a team camp, giving the Canadian riders a chance to unite and try to come together as a cohesive unit. This is quite a large unit including three Dutch Warmblood mares, one Hanovarian gelding, a Friesian stallion, their five riders and two trainers. The support team consists of three grooms, two personal assistants, the team manager, and a massage therapist. (Lauren planned on taking full advantage of her. In fact the first time I met Lauren in person she was on the massage table preparing herself mentally and physically for the grueling competition ahead.) Lauren proudly hangs her Parelli banner there at the Flag is Up Farms where the Canadian flag was also displayed in the area assigned to the Canadian Team.

Lauren brings something else with her to Solvang, the rekindling of an old romance. This romance dated back to Grade Four when Lauren lived in Sointula with her dad. They found each other again on *Facebook*. A single dad with a five year old son, Peter visited while she was in her Canadian quarantine, and he was very supportive of her while she was in Hong Kong. Lauren could chat with him night and day using the computer. It was comforting for Lauren to have face to face conversations with him, but because of the huge time difference between Vancouver Island and Hong Kong, he almost always responded with a sleepy, dazed look. The e mails Peter sent were, as Lauren describes them, out of this world funny, and this kept her spirits up when it was an easy time to be stressed. Even if Lauren didn't want to talk, they would play computer games. Peter would later visit Lauren in Florida, but by September of 2009 he broke up with her. The long distance was just too tough, and Lauren didn't put as much into the relationship as it needed. Lauren doesn't relish conversation as much as she enjoys the companionship of a significant other. She doesn't feel she is very romantic, forgetting an anniversary or even to call. She says she's never been a stellar girlfriend. She knows she has been treated wonderfully, but is very aware a relationship with her can be difficult. And as with other boyfriends, Lauren's focus on her competitive equestrian career interfered with romance.

Maile traveled well to California, but Lauren's trip was not as uneventful, including cancelled airline tickets, her wheelchair hi-jacked, her I-pod stolen, and a wonderful fall off a curb. The hi-jacking of her chair is actually quite funny. Lauren was sitting in the airplane waiting to get off because she always goes on first and gets off last. While looking down at the tarmac, she sees an old man hop into her wheelchair thinking it was an airport chair. All she could do was bang on the window and scream that he was taking her chair! Lauren's chair is quite sporty, and if he had given it a real big push, he would have flipped over. Fortunately,

Sandra was able to sprint off the plane and retrieve it for her.

The good news is her luggage arrived, her body was in good condition, and Maile was glad to see her. Lauren marvels again at how well the mare is handling everything. Lauren describes her as a pro. She was becoming fitter and fitter, more powerful with each ride. Practicing the trot up for the vet exam, Lauren is confident Maile will pass as well as all four other horses on the team. Maile has also proved to be the busy body of the barn, having a bite to eat and then standing with her head outside the stall door to observe everything that was going on. Her social, friendly demeanor lightened the mood of the barn.

This quarantine is extremely strict with no turn-out for the horses. They will be training as a team daily, riding either early in the morning or very late at night so that they can become acclimatized to what they will be dealing with in Hong Kong. Since I live in California and only six hours from Solvang, I asked Lauren if she had a little time during her hectic training schedule to meet with my boyfriend and me. Lauren and I had been talking via e mail and phone about this book, she had answered millions of questions and we'd swapped horse stories. I wanted to meet this person who so fully captivated my life face to face, and I felt she should see the writer, in the flesh, that was going to try and capture her amazing story. We agreed to meet on a Sunday morning just before the horses would be flying out to Hong Kong. Neither of us knew what to expect with the restrictions of the quarantine. I was prepared to be happy just waving to Lauren through a fence and anything in addition to that would be a bonus. Our visit was so much more! I called Lauren on her cell and, as I mentioned, she was on the massage table keeping muscles loose and pliable as athletes need to do. The team manager, Elizabeth, came out to greet us at the gate to the Canadian quarantine area and understandably was a little skeptical. After some explanation, actually not as much as I would have expected, she let us step in a disinfectant solution, wash our hands in disinfectant and enter the quarantine area. We were asked if we had been on any other ranches and fortunately had not. We had eaten a lovely breakfast in Solvang and watched an ostrich mating ritual from the road waiting for The Flag is Up Ranch to open. But, since we had spent the night at friends without horses we were in the clear. We were allowed to go back to the barn with Elizabeth and meet Lauren, Maile, and the whole team, trainers, Sandra and Andrea, and the dedicated support staff. What an honor and a thrill to meet these courageous, funny, and talented women. Riding in the Grade Level lB spot is Ashley Gowanlock, Grade II is Lauren and Jennifer McKenzie, and rounding out the team is Eleonore Elstone and Karen Brain in Grade IV. The equine athletes were amazing as well. A small but fond memory is Maile standing over Lauren in her wheelchair snooping through her Canadian tote bag looking for peppermints while being brushed by Alice her groom. She is an endearing horse.

There was to be no hugging or touching of anything in the area. We were welcome to take pictures, talk with Lauren and the team and soak up the general atmosphere. I would describe this as the calm before the storm. The quarantine environment seemed peaceful, the ranch serene with a focus on horses and training along with a lot of laughs before their final battle for the gold. The conversation ranged from Lauren's roommate Ashley's missing I pod to the roommates eating pizza all night and laughing. We were there talking with the team for several hours and by the time we left, I was in love with this team and their horses. The devotion of the support staff was obvious. Their spirit, camaraderie, professionalism and enthusiasm impressed me greatly. Lauren "walked" us out to the gate, and I wanted to give her a hug but couldn't. She and Maile had touched my heart, and I became a traitor wanting so badly for Team Canada to come home winners. They already were in my mind.

At this time, ride times were being posted on the Beijing Paralympic web site and Lauren could feel the excitement mounting. This was truly becoming real. All the horses accompanied by grooms flew out of Los Angeles the following Tuesday at one o'clock A.M. for a twenty-six hour plane ride that would only stop to refuel in Alaska. They flew longer than horses from any other country competing. Lauren and her team flew back to Canada on the 26th of August and prepared for their long flight out of Vancouver to Hong Kong on the 27th. The end-point of this journey across the skies would find them not only meeting up with their horses but taking the ride of their lifetimes.

Chapter 17

Lauren, arriving in Hong Kong, August 29, 2008, is met by the team manager with a huge smile and an "all's well" with the horses. Maile's vitals were good upon arriving and this left Lauren with only the task of finding her accommodations. She soon realized the "Athlete's Village" was actually a beautifully appointed four star hotel where she was free to rest until the next day. But that next day turned Lauren and Maile's dream upside down. After traveling twenty-six hours by plane, Maile and one other Canadian horse had developed shipping fever, technically pleuropneumonia. It can be deadly. Common among horses that are transported long distances, it is a respiratory infection that affects the lungs and chest cavity. It can be very difficult to treat. Maile was coughing and spiked a fever of 104.3 degrees. The normal body temperature for a horse is ninety-nine to one hundred one degrees. Lauren found Maile in the barn hooked up to IV fluids, receiving antibiotics, being scanned and scoped. She would lose forty-one pounds in five days. The vets held out little hope she would be well enough to participate. Lauren's Paralympic dream seemed to be turning into an effort to keep her horse alive.

Maile reacted well to the treatment and her temperature dropped to one hundred two degrees, but Lauren had two days to get her off the restricted substances so that she could pass a drug test. Her health was more important.

In Lauren's words, "It is really tough to see your partner being so sick and knowing that you put her in that situation compromising her health. I wish I could have explained to her why I had put her on an airplane for twenty-six hours, and that she was in China to help me achieve my goal of eight years. All I could do was feed her an apple and gently rub her belly."

Despite the anguish Lauren was feeling for her horse, Maile was always happy to see her when she came to the barn with apples to feed her. One time the vet came in and saw a frothy substance coming from Maile's mouth and his eyes bulged out. Unbeknownst to him it was apple juice. The veterinarians did agree Maile was their best patient, and they enjoyed treating her the most. This was no relief to Lauren. While the other riders trained, all she could do was walk her mare in hand and let her know that this would most likely be the extent of her Olympic career.

The Paralympic veterinary staff, headed up by Dr. Chris Riggs, worked tirelessly to get the ill horses healthy. Lauren, wanting to do everything possible, went to see the world's second largest Buddha to seek his help. Traveling two and a half hours, Lauren lit two hundred sticks of incense and appealed for the health of the two ill Canadian horses. Four days before the competition, Lauren was given the okay to ride Maile and try to move some of the fluids around in her lungs and see how bad her cough was. The vets stood on the sidelines watching a stressed Lauren and Maile. She received permission to ride very early in the morning and very late at night at the walk. Lauren was able to try her test movements for fifteen minutes. With three days to go, Maile was given conditional approval to do the trot up exam at the veterinary inspection as was the other Canadian horse as long as there was no recurrence of fever or coughing throughout the ride. She was not sure at this point if she could compete, but Lauren was clear that Maile's health was more important than competing.

She says, "There can be more competitions. I was just happy being able to ride her and that she was recovering. "

But she can compete! It is official. September 5th she goes through the trot up exam that all competitors' horses must do. The vets inspect the horse at the walk and trot and make sure they are one hundred per cent sound.

Lauren, frustrated but happy, explains her feelings about her horse and this illness, " You go from being focused on the competition to total focus on keeping her alive and hoping she can just make it home, to it may be possible to pass the vet exam to actually being able to ride again. The fact that I was in the competition ring was more than I could ask from her."

But Lauren did ask, and once again Maile came through with flying colors. Only four of the five horses on the Canadian Team would be allowed to compete in the team portion of the competition. (All five do the individual test.) But Lauren joyously announced on her blog that she and Maile had been named to the team.

"So," Lauren stresses, "I have one more day to prepare Maile. No stress about now! How does four years of thinking about Beijing 2008 turn into counting hours? It is really amazing how time flies. I wish I could get many lost moments back and use them more wisely. To be honest, I have felt very numb over the past week, not wanting to think about what could be or how this week would end. With it all being so close I now feel like I'm ready to explode."

Lauren's life has been a roller coaster ride. Why should the biggest show of a lifetime be any different? She has some preparing to do. Seeing her name on the board with an actual ride time stops her in her tracks. It is actually going to happen. She almost can't believe that all the worries, the stress, the paper work, overanalyzing, reanalyzing, crying, laughing and sleepless nights will come down to six minutes in a ring with five judges from around the world.

During her first training session, after all this reality settles in, Lauren notices that Maile does not have her usual strength, but she has so much heart and try. It brings Lauren to tears realizing how hard her mare is trying knowing she was so ill just days, hours ago. Following Lauren resuming riding Maile, the horse comes out of the stall with legs that are swollen like tree trunks having no definition at all. Lauren empathizes with her since she really looks like her rider at the end of the day. Alice, Maile's groom, thought wrapping her legs would keep down the swelling. But the next morning after wrapping her legs the night before, Alice is horrified to see Maile in the same place she had left her. The shavings hadn't moved. Realizing that some horses do this when their legs are wrapped, Alice began to soak Maile's legs in large tubs of ice water. In addition, Maile will now have a daily ritual of standing in the misters with two cold hoses running down her legs and Lauren will try to get her feet elevated, that is when she is not having fun with Ashley.

They have been maneuvering through a shopping mall attached to their hotel and eating on the largest floating restaurant in the world when not training for the Paralympic Games. One tradition they have continued as roommates across the globe is getting into trouble and doing a lot of giggling about it. This trip starts with a typical Lauren and Ashley evening. Ashley's scooter arrived broken so when they got it back to the room, Lauren tried to take a good look at it.

They both made the decision to plug it in to the charge box in the wall thinking they had the correct adapter for it. As the scooter is making a horrible sound, Ashley yells at Lauren to unplug it. She does while the charger box which was in her lap goes "pop", shooting out a cloud of sparks, fire and smoke. Lauren is not sure if this was a funny event or not, but at the time it caused hysterical laughter to follow. Lauren says no worries; she only suffered a minor burn.

Ashley's scooter recovered but couldn't be charged because the charger for it blew up. Lauren went to the barn with a totally different adapter fuse and voltage converter and plugged her chair in. Poof! Smoke was billowing in the middle of the barn. Now Lauren doesn't have a charger and Ashley doesn't have a charger. They will both soon be "on foot". This leads to even more problems if that is possible.

Lauren has the nifty idea that she can hold onto Ashley's scooter and be towed around. Sitting behind Ashley in a hallway of the hotel, talking on her cell phone and holding onto Ashley's scooter, Lauren realizes Ashley is trying to get her jacket on although it looks more like she is wrestling with a straight jacket. Lauren says "tally ho" and their therapist, Erin, decides to drive the scooter for Ashley while she gets her arms free. The scooter, with a seeming mind of its own, takes off, does a wheelie and launches both Ashley and Lauren into walls, Lauren head first. This is all inspiration for more fits of giggles.

The laughter and camaraderie is part of being a team, and the team test is coming up. Lauren has not even prepared herself for competition thinking, just four days before, that being in the competition ring wasn't even a possibility. But she knows her mare has heart and soul and spirit and no matter what, they will do their best together for each other and Team Canada.

LAUREN AND ASHLEY

Chapter 18

At the age of twenty-two Lauren's back and dreams were shattered. A few days short of her thirty-first birthday, this beautiful young woman now proudly sits astride her beautiful horse entering the competition arena for Team Canada hoping to change the course of her personal history and her country's. It is actually going to happen; Lauren and Maile are going to compete on Sunday, the seventh of September, at 8:49 a.m., with eight of her family members looking on, aunts and uncles and Ray and Robin, all watching her with love and pride. Seeing her ride time displayed on the board, Lauren experiences silence, fear and then panic. She had to completely change her frame of mind from not knowing if she was going to compete to, "I am going in that ring!"

Lauren remembers the three days leading up to the first day of competition as a blur with Saturday before the competition taking the honors for the most hiccups. She remembers trying to have a bath but the water system in the hotel was acting up. She had set the water for a pleasant luke-warm temperature and left it to fill up. Assuming the temperature was what she set it for, she dropped her feet into the tub, and they bounced right back out. The water was scalding hot. Thankful there were no blisters, she went down to the internet to e mail the Parellis and the internet was down. Thinking she could use her cell phone to call out, she found out that her American Verizon cell phone only wanted to call home to Canada. But, she still had options. She could use the pay phone on the second floor. The pay phone took her credit card and kept it. She actually had to go to the first floor to find someone who could remove her credit card from the phone. Lauren doesn't give up easily, so she then tried to call out by punching her credit card number into the phone. This seemed to work until she was notified that her credit card had been frozen. Continuing with determination, Lauren used her cell phone to call the 800 number for the credit card company and was put on hold for ten minutes. Someone finally came on the phone and while confirming her personal information, her phone went dead. Now more than mildly frustrated and temporarily lacking common sense, Lauren returned to the pay phone to put in another credit card expecting a different result. This card was kept too. Feeling rather foolish, Lauren reappeared on the first floor seeking assistance. With help, she did make her call with a calling card, every two seconds of call time equaling one Canadian dollar!

It's now time to get dressed and get ready to ride Maile. Lauren arrives at the elevator only to discover it is broken and won't come get her. One of the four elevators had its alarm going off. Being on the fifteenth floor, all of a sudden, became a little scary. One of the British assistants took the fifteen flights of stairs down to get help. Ten minutes later, Lauren was riding the elevator but with grave reservations. Being trapped on the fifteenth floor sounded so much better than being trapped in an elevator. Nevertheless she made it down.

Power mobility for both Lauren and Ashley became manual after all the charger problems upon arriving with their wheelchairs. They had three different convertors and none of them seemed to work. These are the difficulties of everyday life that intruded into their glamorous Paralympic world. Overcoming these obstacles and the huge obstacle of her horse's health, Lauren and Maile did make it through another day of schooling and believe they will be good to go for competing the next day.

Unusual for her, Lauren woke up extremely nervous on her first day of competition. She was out of her element unable to deal with it. Jittery and needing to move, she felt like exploding and couldn't focus. Fortunately her day started at 3:30 a.m. with stretching and therapy for her neck and shoulders. Then she was off dressed in her competition whites with her hair braided and madly stuffing her things in a bag. Needing to eat, she zipped through the cafeteria grabbing anything that didn't require utensils. Of course this would mean an overload on carbs, two croissants, one blueberry muffin and a banana. Not a breakfast of champions, but it would have to do. While she was on the shuttle bus she tried to close her eyes and visualize her ride, typical preparation for a competition. Instead of the productive visualization session she had hoped for, her mind wandered to some pretty irrelevant thoughts; did she turn off her flat iron, did she make her bed, how many calories are in two croissants, did she put on her beige underwear that don't show under her white riding pants? When she arrived at the barn she found Maile braided, clean and looking stunning. This was good. But when Andrea, the national coach asked Lauren how she was doing, Lauren burst out in tears.

With a weak voice she said, "I don't know what to do. I am so nervous, and I just don't know how to handle it."

In eight years Lauren had never felt like this and it was making her crazy. Lots of hugs and reassurance from the team helped, and she put herself to work to keep busy. She could put on her riding hat, riding boots, stock tie, riding gloves and check her knee rolls and straps. Oops, no stock tie! Frantically, Lauren searched her bag and found silk panties instead. She had a minor panic attack envisioning herself riding down the center line with underwear wrapped around her neck. Fortunately a fellow teammate had hers at the barn and didn't compete until later. Going to a quiet place in the barn with her borrowed stock tie, Lauren tried to focus again and ten minutes later, before her test, she was in the indoor warm up ring feeling a little better. She still felt like throwing up and her mind was still fuzzy, but Maile felt great! Four minutes before moving to the outdoor five minute ring and doing some medium trots, some halts, she puts on her riding jacket. This is it!

Lauren and Maile enter the main arena trotting around the outside of the ring past all of the judges booths. Maile suddenly becomes elevated and very expressive, too expressive. Her legs and tail are out of control! Quietly telling Maile she is a good girl, she doesn't need all this extra stuff, Lauren convinces both of them to relax. They did a practice halt, taking deep breaths, and the bell sounded. One minute to go until competition. As Lauren looked up and around to line herself up with the center line, everything became clear. Her focus was back.

The ride was over before she knew it. She didn't even hear the lovely music in the background. One minute Lauren and Maile were heading down the center line to begin their team test and the next minute they were halting and saluting, signaling the end. Their ride was steady and accurate, scoring in the high sixties. Lauren was the second rider leaving her a torturous two hours to sit and wait. During the awful wait, she was interviewed twice and handled the interviews well, not mentioning any of the no no's; pollution, human rights, or Tibet. She held on to the first place position until the second to the last rider. She was shocked to see how low the other scores were. The arena at the Sha Tin venue, where the equestrian games were staged, had been causing problems for many of the riders with decorations of giant panda bears peeking out from behind bamboo and trees that looked like dragons. The results board was huge and electric and around the arena were flowers, wells, waterfalls, statues and the Olympic Torch. Horses were spooking left, right and center and causing quite a scare for the spectators. Lauren was thinking about what a great foundation she and Maile had and their experiences at the Parelli ranch. Those cows that Maile had to learn to love turned out to be a blessing in disguise. By the end of the first day of competition, Lauren found herself in second place, and she had given Team Canada a great start. She was ecstatic knowing that she and Maile had done their best. She had watched as other riders' horses were tense and afraid of the arena, and had seen so many mistakes. Proud that she had put in a solid performance, she was sad knowing the rest of the riders still had their best to perform.

Lauren was more than satisfied. The fact that she was in the competition ring exceeded what Lauren felt she could ask of Maile. She showed so much heart and character that Lauren couldn't help but think about how fortunate she was to have been able to develop a partnership with her. And true to her character, Maile gave even more. On September 9, 2008, Lauren and Maile won silver in the Grade II Individual Championship Test. With a score of 68.454, they finished just behind Britta Naepel of Germany. This was Lauren's first Paralympic medal. This was what she had dreamed of and worked for.

Waiting to hear the results the day she won silver was almost as difficult as winning it. Lauren was one of the first riders and there were lots of riders to follow her. She felt she had put in a decent test, but she didn't think it was a winning score. She went to the international tent to watch the remaining riders and that was hard. Rider after rider went and their horses were spooking, bolting and leaving the arena. Lauren was shocked that with six riders left to go she remained in second place. Unsettling thoughts of how Maile would have done if she had been one hundred per cent swirled around in her head. Finishing even in the top five seemed like a miracle, but she was beside herself wondering, "what if?" Someone in the tent noticed that she was nervous and aghast at what she was seeing, so he suggested, "You need a beer!" He bought her a can of Chinese beer. Lauren drank it, and realized that two riders later she was still in second place. And most importantly, she was not in fourth! Fourth place would be heartbreakingly close. Another rider went and Lauren realized that she had at least won the bronze and found another complimentary beer in front of her. She cracked it open, took a couple of sips and suddenly realized it was barely 9:00 A.M., and she had won a silver medal and drank a beer and a half! She wheeled straight out to Maile without stopping to see anyone. With tears in her eyes she thanked her magnificent mare.

She could only say, "To actually have that medal, it makes the eight years feel like I was doing something right."

The reality took a while to set in, but she did have the medal around her neck to prove it to herself and the world. Maile had done it. She had not only competed while being ill, but Lauren believed she gave her the silver medal, way beyond what she had expected. Her heart and courage are huge, Lauren knew, but she didn't realize how much Maile had to give until she gave it all to her.

Maile and Lauren impressed a few other people too. Elizabeth Quigg-Robinson, the Canadian Para-Dressage

Chef d'equipe or national team manager, remarked, "We are ecstatic with the result; this is a great medal for Canada. Lauren's silver medal was a great team effort."

Akaash Maharaj, Equine Canada's CEO, continues, "By bringing a medal at the first possible opportunity, Lauren has re-affirmed Canada's place as one of the foremost Para-Equestrian nations in the world. We are tremendously proud of her, her achievement at the Paralympics and her success in raising the bar for all athletes across Canada and across international equestrianism."

After getting up at five o'clock the morning of the silver, Lauren was exhausted. Her immediate plans were to sleep for as long as she could. After the medal ceremony, Lauren came to the conclusion that she didn't want to continue competing. She felt Maile had given her everything she had to offer, and she should not ask for anything more. She thought about quitting while she was ahead, the perfect time. She would thank Maile for all she had done and be satisfied. She had captured the elusive medal.

Thoughts bouncing around in her brain went something like this, "When you have a dream, it turns into your goal. Sometimes that goal turns your dream into what feels like a nightmare. Over the past year, I have had many frustrations causing me to shed tears, causing me to re-evaluate my dream. I always kept coming back to the same conclusion that it is what I want and it is worth many sacrifices. To 'ride for the gold' is what I said back in 2001. When I didn't achieve that in Athens I remember saying that it was okay. I hadn't failed; I just hadn't reached my final target yet. As I continued to journey towards my goal, I changed my direction many times, but all with the same expected outcome."

Feeling as if she may have achieved that outcome, she has doubts about continuing on in the Freestyle Competition. With encouragement from her teammates who had all seen her practice her freestyle, observing that she was an excellent freestyle rider and had wonderful music and choreography, Lauren felt she needed to see the Buddha again. Remembering the positive result from her first trip, Lauren retraced her journey and thanked the Buddha for his intervention. She decided to go for it and ride in the Freestyle Competition.

Chapter 19

Changing her attitude from earlier competitions and dismissing nervousness and the need to focus on perfection, Lauren decided to change course and to have fun. She was going to go into the ring and dance to music with her partner, Maile. The Freestyle Test lends itself more to this frame of mind. The riders can create their own pattern of movements called a floor plan. The plan does have to incorporate compulsory movements as defined by the IPEC, but the test is ridden to music that the rider chooses to match and enhance the paces of the horse. This test shows the unity between rider and horse through rhythm and harmony in the movements and transitions.

Lauren's music that she describes as "sort of like an ode to China" was the perfect choice for she and Maile. Lauren prefers to ride to more powerful music, but her choreographer in Vancouver, Karen Robinson, thought there was just no way that kind of music would fit Maile. Karen felt the crowd would love the Asian choice and they did. The judges were enchanted as well. The floodlit arena was filled with the exuberance of the personalities of both horse and rider performing with a breathtaking show of walks and trots perfectly timed to the music.

Nearly eight years after being forced to get back on a horse, Lauren and Maile win the gold late on Wednesday night, September 10, 2008. She says she will be "forever grateful to those who gave her back her choice." Her score was 72.7766 placing her on top of sixteen other riders, but this can't begin to describe the magnitude of this moment for both Lauren and Team Canada.

Lauren graciously remarks, "All my friends, team members and sponsors have allowed me the opportunity to succeed. But most importantly, I have had the honor to ride a horse with a lot of heart."

This gold medal marks the first equestrian gold medal ever for Canada in the Paralympic Games and, for Lauren; it is the culmination of eight years of hard work and dedication to her sport.

Equine Canada's CEO again lavishly compliments Lauren by saying, "Lauren's gold medal is an achievement of epic proportions. This is not simply our country's first-ever Paralympics gold medal. It makes our equestrian medal achievements at the 2008 Summer Games greater than that from all previous Summer Games combined over the entire 122 year history of modern Olympism. We are immensely grateful to Lauren and the broader Canadian Equestrian Team for ushering in Canada's golden age of Olympic and Paralympic equestrianism."

Yes, she danced that night with her fantastic partner to new age oriental music and won a gold medal. Looking at her score that night she knew she had won at least the silver, however there was still a German rider who had beaten her before left to ride.

When Lauren discovered she was in first place and her score hadn't been beaten, all she could say was, "No, no way, no it is not possible!!"

But it was. Filled with disbelief and shock, Lauren was lacking words. She wants to explain how she feels, but she really believes no one can understand the depth of emotion of this moment without experiencing it.

After winning the gold medal, Lauren returns from the stable at 12:30 a.m. In her blog she simply states, "Maile and I won a gold medal tonight in our freestyle. It's amazing and I'm lost for words."

But returning to the United States after the medal ceremonies and all the accompanying excitement of the Summer Paralympics and China, Lauren does have time to reflect on where she is at this point in time and where she is going. For sure she knows that Pat Parelli and Walter Zettl helped Maile to go to China with a solid foundation, giving her that competitive edge, allowing her to be stronger mentally and emotionally especially since she was weak physically. In the three months since she left the Parelli Ranch for Canada, Lauren and Maile have experienced strict quarantine, limited training times, travel to California for more quarantine, flights to and from Hong Kong, shipping fever and three amazing days of competition.

Describing the journey as the, "ultimate test of physical, emotional and mental fitness for both Maile and me. Maile showed me the depth that a horse's heart can reach. "

Talking with one of her mentors after her return, Lauren discussed being uncomfortable with the role of being an inspiration to others. She feels inwardly uncomfortable and outwardly awkward when other people reveal to her that they are motivated or inspired by her accomplishments. Thinking about this for a while, Lauren discovered this came from her lack of desire to do what she does for recognition or acknowledgment from others. As incredible as it is to have won a silver and gold medal, the knowledge that she is being the best that she can be is her highest reward. She loves being challenged and the thrill of doing something she has worked for. She derives pleasure from knowing that every day she has progressed and that each day brings her closer to being better, and ultimately being her best. Understanding this, she accepts the role of being an inspiration and helping people become empowered to achieve great things or just fulfill their smallest goals. Like it or not, Lauren is a role model. She hopes she can live up to that.

Meanwhile back at the Parelli Ranch, Lauren is awarded her black string by Pat himself. The levels of the program are red, blue, green and black. Quite an honor. This represents outstanding achievement at a high level of performance with your horse. Linda Parelli writes in the *Savvy Times*, the official magazine of Parelli Natural Horsemanship, that Lauren won the gold, "because she had decided to do it for fun and didn't care about winning. What an incredible demonstration of principle under the most pressing of conditions. It's not about the...medal, the win, the prize, the ego...it's all about the confidence, the preparation, the excellence, the mental and emotional fitness...the trust...the relationship."

Lauren adds to Linda's comments by saying, "Looking back, all the Parelli Keys to Success were there for me: attitude, technique, tools, knowledge, imagination, time and support."

Lauren continues with compliments for Maile, "It's a special relationship. I need to buy her. She's got so much heart and spirit. I want to continue on with her." Dreaming of her future, Lauren would like to be the first paralyzed rider to ride Grand Prix dressage. She also envisions owning a farm to train horses for people with disabilities. She believes that her two medals will help to open the eyes of horse owners that riders like herself can be competitive with the right type of horse.

She is also giving out bonus points for people who say something other than "congratulations" to her. Her favorite so far is "superbly done". Her life journey to date has been superbly done but as have so many journeys to greatness, Lauren's has taken a circuitous route. Her dream of becoming an elite athlete in the equestrian world was accomplished, but not in a way she would have ever imagined. Nevertheless, she did it. She rode for and seized the gold!

ELIZABETH QUIGG-ROBINSON, SANDRA VERDA, LAUREN AND MAILE WINNING GOLD

Happy Team Canada

Epilogue

Wheeling through an adoring, enthusiastic crowd, Lauren returns to Langley, Canada, to carry the torch and light the Olympic cauldron for the 2010 Winter Games. With a glowing smile and dressed all in white including her cap, Lauren feels the appreciation and honor her home country affords her. She is a star! She pulls a wheelie and circles her chair with almost childlike exuberance knowing how far she has come on her journey. She started in Canada and it has come full circle. She is only here for a few days, taking a time-out from her competition schedule, but her welcome is everything she deserves. She has deep roots in this community, and the community knows this.

The chair of the Langley Torch Relay Committee, Jordan Bateman, feels, "She epitomizes what Langley is all about. Through her hard work and determination, she has overcome tremendous hardship to follow her dream and become a world champion. She was the natural choice for this honour."

She responds, "It is huge for me in the sense that Langley is the horse capital of B. C. and so much of what I have accomplished is because the people of Langley have supported me. A lot of people that were part of my journey never got to be at my event, so for them to get to experience this excitement with me is great."

Many of her friends and family are here with their full support to cheer her on. The crowd totals 16,000. The date is February 8, 2010, and she will carry the flame to the Langley Events Centre and light the cauldron. Lauren was chosen from a pool of candidates by the Torch Relay Committee.

Responding to this selection, she says, "I was completely shocked and surprised to be asked to carry the torch. Being able to carry the Olympic torch and to be a part of that special journey is the next best thing to being able to compete, but I had an odd feeling about mounting fire to my wheel chair."

Just prior to this honor, Lauren was awarded the Inaugural Equine Canada's President Award. Lauren was selected not only as Canada's most successful Para-Equestrian athlete in history, but as a powerful ambassador for equestrian sport. Lauren is considered a leader and a role model in the equestrian community worldwide. She has been Equine Canada's official spokesperson for Horse Week 2009. She assists younger athletes with their competitive pursuits, sharing her experience, and offering a unique perspective as an athlete. Because of her contributions as a competitor, trainer and mentor, and for reaching the highest pinnacle of success in her sport, she was not only awarded but celebrated at the Equine Canada Annual Awards Gala on Saturday, February 6, 2010, in Ottawa.

The journey is not over. Lauren has purchased Maile. She performs and speaks at Parelli Celebrations making her Parelli sponsors proud, she has become a Four Star Parelli Instructor and she will be going to the World Equestrian

Games this year, 2010, in Kentucky. Continuing to compete internationally, she will most likely be there in London in 2012 at the Summer Paralympic Games, demonstrating not only excellence of performance but greatness of spirit.

Lauren's coach Sandra Verda once said words to Lauren that carried her to Paralympic glory. She said, "To achieve greatness in any sport requires natural ability combined with many hours of dedication, often sacrificing many of life's pleasures in order to attain that extra ounce of peak performance that sets you apart from other competitors. As this journey unfolds it becomes more and more obvious that so much of what we do, so many of our successes and experiences whether positive or negative, are determined by our minds. Lauren, you are a prime example of how obstacles can be overcome by determination, hard work and a positive attitude."

We will see her ride for gold again. She believes and makes us all believe that she will achieve all her goals and her dreams. The cauldron is lit, the flame burns on, and the continuing struggle to overcome adversity and be triumphant never ends.

LAUREN AND MAILE WIN GOLD

To Cindy,
Thanks for being
~~a~~ apart of the journey.
Lots of short sessions'!

Made in the USA
Charleston, SC
19 August 2011